DEAR GROWN-UPS,

Summer is full of opportunities to play and learn and we want to make it easy to find inspiring, kid-friendly activities! That's why we've worked with PBS stations and content creators from across the country to bundle up some of our favorite activities into one, easy-to-carry-any-where book. We hope you and your kids will use this to inspire learning all summer long!

Here are a few quick tips to keep your kids excited about learning this summer:

- **ASK LOTS OF QUESTIONS**. Encourage your kids to participate in conversations by asking them questions like: Why do you think that happened? What will happen next?

- **ENCOURAGE KIDS TO SEARCH FOR ANSWERS**. When your children ask you "why?" see if you can work together to figure out what they need to know or do to find the answer.

- **TRY SOMETHING NEW**. Summer is a great time to try new things like reading a new kind of book, tasting a new food or exploring a new park.

- **JUST HAVE FUN**. Summertime only comes along once a year, so be sure to take the time to relax and have fun while you're learning.

- **BUILD LASTING, POSITIVE MEMORIES THAT WILL LAST A LIFETIME!**

HOW TO USE THIS BOOK

- Keep in mind that this book spans multiple grade levels. Your child won't be using every single page, but choosing a few lessons each week. The goal is to keep kids' brains engaged with a taste of reading, writing, math, art, science, and physical activity every week.

- The grade levels are merely guides to get you started. We recommend starting with the grade that your child just completed and adjusting as needed. Don't be shy about using a different grade level or just picking and choosing lessons that look interesting. This has been a tough year for our children and we want your child to feel proud and confident.

- This book aligns with the content on the Michigan Learning Channel, which can be used on live tv or on demand. There are about 2-3 hours a week of video lessons, plus lots of activities in this book that don't use a screen. We recommend getting outside everyday, reading everyday and having enjoyable moments together as a family!

- This book is designed to use for 8 weeks of summer. We suggest spreading it out over a few days each week and finding a time that works for your family. If you have older children they may do better in the evenings.

- As you go through the weeks, you will find each week has a theme and a link to videos that go with the activities. You can find all the video lessons, plus interactive virtual events and more at **www.michiganlearning.org/summer**.

How do the students in your life use the Michigan Learning Channel? We would love your feedback! Feel free to contact us at mlc@dptv.org.

Michigan Learning Channel Team
MichiganLearning.org

Dates and Themes

The summer program runs from June 20 to August 14, 2022.
Each week has a set of lessons, plus additional programs, activities, and field trips based on the weekly theme.

Take Flight (June 20-26):
From planes and kites to butterflies and birds, discover the fables and physics of things that fly.

Under Water (June 27-July 3):
Dive deep into oceans, rivers, and our own Great Lakes to discover what it takes to live beneath the waves.

Heroes (July 4-10):
Celebrate our nation's birthday and the people we call heroes, whether they are veterans, everyday helpers, or the kind who wear capes.

Creatures (July 11-17):
From the prehistoric to the present, learn about the fascinating features of creatures near and far.

Engineering (July 18-24):
Meet the people who design bridges, cars, and video games and learn how to think like an engineer.

Great Outdoors (July 25-31):
Explore the world outside your door and the incredible parks and waters that belong to us all.

When I Grow Up (August 1-7):
All summer we'll learn about different careers—this week, think about all the exciting possibilities in your future!

Shoot for the Stars (August 8-14):
Look up at the night sky and into outer space and meet people who risked everything to follow their dreams.

On TV. Online. Statewide.

Learn more about the Michigan Learning Channel at
Facebook Live at fb.me/michlearning
www.michiganlearning.org/summer

 Follow @MichLearning on social media to find out more.

rev 2/22

Where to Find the Michigan Learning Channel

Find your favorite shows anywhere you go!

Scan the QR Code:
Scan any of the QR codes in this book to see the accompanying video right on your device.

On Demand:
Video lessons and activities at MichiganLearning.org

Click your grade level for this week's selected lessons

Or, use "Find a Lesson" to search by grade, subject, and educational standard

On the App:
Find shows on the free PBS app

The PBS App is available for mobile devices, Roku, Apple TV, and on many Smart TVs.

Search for Read Write Roar, Math Mights, Extra Credit, DIY Science Time, Wimee's Words, InPACT at Home, Simple Gift Series, and more great programs.

On the Livestream:
Watch the 24/7 livestream at MichiganLearning.org/live-tv

On TV:
Find us on broadcast television with an antenna

Coming soon to:
Charter Cable services in Northern Michigan and the Upper Peninsula.
Visit MichiganLearning.org/Schedule for details

On TV. Online. Statewide.

Learn more about the Michigan Learning Channel at
Facebook Live at fb.me/michlearning
www.michiganlearning.org/summer

 Follow @MichLearning on social media to find out more.

The Michigan Learning Channel is funded through a grant awarded by the Michigan Department of Education and the U.S. Department of Education.

Michigan LEARNING CHANNEL
A PUBLIC MEDIA PARTNERSHIP

Serving Schools Statewide
Through Your Local PBS Stations

Watch On-Demand at
MichiganLearning.org

f 𝕏 📷 **@MichLearning**

**The Michigan Learning Channel
is Available On:**

WCMU
Alpena Channel 6.4

Cadillac
Channel 27.4

Manistee
Channel 21.4

Mt. Pleasant
Channel 14.4

Shelby Shawl
Shelby.shawl@cmich.edu

WDCQ
Delta College Public Media
Channel 19.5

Lauren Saj
laurensaj@delta.edu
(989) 686-9346

WGVU
Grand Rapids
Channel 35.6

Kalamazoo
Channel 52.6
Rachel Cain
cainra@gvsu.edu

WKAR
WKAR Public Media
Channel 23.5
Summer Godette, M.Ed,
summer@wkar.org
(517) 884-4700

WNMU
WNMU-TV
Channel 13.4
Ellen Doan
WNMU Public Media
edoan@nmu.edu
(906) 227-6765

WTVS
Detroit Public TV
Channel 56.5
Olivia Misterovich
omisterovich@dptv.org

WNIT
Michiana PBS
Channel 34.5
Sheri Robertson
srobertson@wnit.org
Cass and Berrien
counties

COMING SOON
to Charter Cable in
Northern and Mid-Michigan
and the Upper Peninsula

Rescan Your TV to watch on Broadcast

Your remote control and TV menus may vary, but the steps
are the same. Your TV will scan for all available channels.

TV sets connected to cable, satellite or other pay TV
providers do not need to scan.

How to Scan
1. Press menu on your remote control.
2. Select setup.
3. Choose antenna then channel scan
   or auto tune.

rev 2/22

WEEKDAY SUMMER SCHEDULE

TIME	GRADE	WHAT'S ON
5AM	Preschool - Kindergarten	Let's Learn
6AM		PBS Kids shows
6:30AM		Wimee's Words, Simple Gifts Series
7AM		Let's Learn
8AM		Read, Write, ROAR! (Kindergarten)
8:30AM		Math Mights (Kindergarten)
9AM	1st - 3rd Grade	Read, Write, ROAR! (1st Grade)
9:30AM		Math Mights (1st Grade)
10AM		Read, Write, ROAR! (2nd Grade)
10:30AM		Math Mights (2nd Grade)
11AM		Read, Write, ROAR! (3rd Grade)
11:30AM		Math Mights (3rd Grade)
12PM		Live From the City Opera House: It's Storytime
12:30PM		PBS Kids shows
1PM	4th - 6th Grade	Extra Credit
1:30PM		Math & Movement
2PM		Story Pirates
2:30PM		DIY Science Time, SciGirls
3PM		Curious Crew
3:30PM	1st - 3rd Grade	Cyberchase, Into the Outdoors
4PM		Read, Write, ROAR! (2nd & 3rd Grade)
4:30PM		Math Mights (2nd & 3rd Grade)
5PM	Preschool - Kindergarten	Read, Write, ROAR! (Kindergarten & 1st Grade)
5:30PM		Math Mights (Kindergarten & 1st Grade)
6PM		Let's Learn
7PM	4th - 6th Grade	Extra Credit
7:30PM		Math & Movement
8PM		Story Pirates
8:30PM		DIY Science Time, SciGirls
9PM 5AM	6th - 12th Grade	Nature, NOVA, American Experience, Ken Burns and other PBS programming

Details at MichiganLearning.org/schedule

rev 02/22

WATCH on the Michigan Learning Channel.
Episodes are available on-demand or stream the channel at
MichiganLearning.org/summer

Visit MichiganLearning.org
and follow @MichLearning
on social media to find out more.

Learn at Home with PBS KIDS

Schedule Begins October 4, 2021

Explore reading, math, science, life lessons, and more on the PBS KIDS 24/7 channel and live stream!
The TV schedule below offers you and your child a chance to learn anytime alongside your friends from PBS KIDS.

TIME (M-F)	SHOW	GRADE	LEARNING GOALS
6/5c am	The Cat in the Hat Knows a Lot About That!	PK-1	Science & Engineering
6:30/5:30c am	Ready Jet Go!	K-2	Science & Engineering
7/6c am	Peg + Cat	PK-K	Math
7:30/6:30c am	Super WHY!	PK-K	Literacy
8/7c am	Daniel Tiger's Neighborhood	PK-K	Social & Emotional Learning
8:30/7:30c am	Daniel Tiger's Neighborhood	PK-K	Social & Emotional Learning
9/8c am	Sesame Street	PK-K	Literacy, Math, Social & Emotional Learning
9:30/8:30c am	Elinor Wonders Why	PK-K	Science & Engineering
10/9c am	Clifford the Big Red Dog	PK-K	Social & Emotional Learning, Literacy
10:30/9:30c am	Dinosaur Train	PK-K	Science
11/10c am	Let's Go Luna!	K-2	Social Studies
11:30/10:30c am	Curious George	PK-K	Math, Science & Engineering
12 pm/11c am	Nature Cat	K-3	Science
12:30 pm/11:30c am	Xavier Riddle and the Secret Museum	K-2	Social & Emotional Learning
1/12c pm	Molly of Denali	K-2	Literacy
1:30/12:30c pm	Hero Elementary	K-2	Science & Engineering
2/1c pm	Cyberchase	1-5	Math & Science
2:30/1:30c pm	Pinkalicious & Peterrific	PK-1	The Arts
3/2c pm	Pinkalicious & Peterrific	PK-1	The Arts
3:30/2:30c pm	Elinor Wonders Why	PK-K	Science & Engineering
4/3c pm	Donkey Hodie	PK-K	Social & Emotional Learning
4:30/3:30c pm	Curious George	PK-K	Math, Science & Engineering
5/4c pm	Alma's Way	K-1	Social & Emotional Learning
5:30/4:30c pm	Xavier Riddle and the Secret Museum	K-2	Social & Emotional Learning
6/5c pm	Molly of Denali	K-2	Literacy
6:30/5:30c pm	Hero Elementary	K-2	Science & Engineering

Access FREE, at-home learning activities, tips, and more on pbskidsforparents.org

LIVE Virtual Events

As part of the Summer Program, students can participate in live virtual events via Facebook Live. Events are interactive and presenters will take student suggestions and questions in real time. Recorded versions of these events will also be available online.

Live virtual events will be hosted on the Michigan Learning Channel Facebook page.

Wimee's Words Live!

Recommended for ages 4-8

Join the loveable robot puppet Wimee and his friends as they discover more about the weekly theme. Wimee needs your help to write stories! Give Wimee your favorite words and ideas in the comments and watch as he incorporates them into stories and songs in real time. Your ideas may even be featured in future episodes of "Wimee's Words" on PBS!

**Wimee's Words Live! with the Michigan Learning Channel
Every Wednesday, June 21-August 9, 4pm
Live on the Michigan Learning Channel Facebook page**

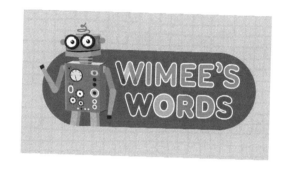

Great Lakes Now Watch Party with the Belle Isle Aquarium

Recommended for ages 8 and up

The monthly PBS show *Great Lakes Now* explores the water, people, and environmental issues that tie together the whole Great Lakes basin. Once a month, they team up with the Belle Isle Aquarium to take a deep dive into the themes of the show. Students will have the chance to ask questions of the guest scientists and meet fantastic fish and other creatures.

Great Lakes Now **Watch Party
Friday, July 1, 1pm
Friday, August 5, 1pm
Live on the Michigan Learning Channel Facebook page**

On TV. Online.
Statewide.

Learn more about the Michigan Learning Channel at
**Facebook Live at fb.me/michlearning
www.michiganlearning.org/summer**

Follow @MichLearning on social media to find out more.

Learn Anywhere!
On Air. Online. On Demand.

Serving students statewide through your local PBS station, the Michigan Learning Channel has everything kids need to build their brains and engage in learning key concepts to succeed in school!

Preschool
Read, sing, and play with your little one.

Wimee's Words
Join Wimee, the fun, lovable robot that inspires kids to learn through creativity.

Simple Gift Series
Make music, find something new, and read with Betty the Bookworm.

POP Check
Mindful practice tools to Pause, Own what we are feeling, and Practice relaxing.

Kindergarten to 3rd Grade
Keep kids learning with fun lessons taught by Michigan teachers.

Read, Write, Roar
Kids build literacy skills with engaging ELA lessons.

Math Mights
Build number sense and learn strategies for solving math problems.

InPACT
Get moving with this home-based physical activity program.

4th to 6th Grade
Short, engaging videos and hands-on lessons keep tweens engaged.

Extra Credit
Creative writing, math, fitness, career exploration, and more!

Curious Crew
Dr. Rob Stephensen and inquisitive kids take a hands-on apprach to scientific exploration.

Story Pirates
Bite-sized literary lessons with comedians, authors, and teachers.

VISIT us online to view all shows, learn about events, and download activities!
www.michiganlearning.org
Follow @michlearning to find out more.

Learn at Home with PBS KIDS

Play and learn anytime and anywhere with free apps from PBS KIDS! Use the chart below to find the app that aligns to your child's grade, learning goal, and favorite PBS KIDS show - then download it on your on your mobile or tablet device to play online, offline, or anytime.

Apps for Social & Emotional Learning

Daniel Tiger for Parents	PK-K	Social & Emotional Learning
PBS KIDS Games app	K-2	Multiple Learning Goals
PBS KIDS Video app	K-2	Multiple Learning Goals

Apps for Literacy Learning

Dinosaur Train A to Z	PK-K	Literacy, Science
Molly of Denali	K-2	Literacy
PBS KIDS Games app	K-2	Multiple Learning Goals
PBS KIDS Video app	K-2	Multiple Learning Goals

Apps for STEM Learning (Science, Technology, Engineering & Math)

PBS Parents Play & Learn	PK-K	Literacy, Math	Photo Stuff with Ruff	K-2	Science
Play & Learn Engineering	PK-K	Science and Engineering	Ready Jet Go! Space Explorer	K-2	Science
PBS KIDS Measure Up!	PK-K	Math	Ready Jet Go! Space Scouts	K-2	Science and Engineering
Play & Learn Science	PK-K	Science	Nature Cat's Great Outdoors	K-3	Science
Splash and Bubbles for Parents	PK-K	Science	PBS KIDS ScratchJr	1-2	Coding
Splash and Bubbles Ocean Adventure	PK-K	Science	Outdoor Family Fun with Plum	1-3	Science and Engineering
The Cat in the Hat Builds That!	PK-K	Science and Engineering	Cyberchase Shape Quest	1-5	Math
The Cat in the Hat Invents	PK-K	Science and Engineering	PBS KIDS Games app	K-2	Multiple Learning Goals
Jet's Bot Builder: Robot Games	K-2	Science and Engineering	PBS KIDS Video app	K-2	Multiple Learning Goals

 **pbskids.org/apps**

Week 1: Take Flight

June 20-26

From planes and kites to butterflies and birds, discover the fables and physics of things that fly.

Use the sheet below to mark off this week's activities as you complete them. See if you can get a BINGO!

Playlists this week: www.michiganlearning.org/takeflight

Be a pollinator with Cyberchase	60 mins. of activity	Read 20 minutes	Make paper airplanes with Ready, Jet, GO!	Watch Read, Write, ROAR!
Read 20 minutes	Watch Math Mights	Look for birds	Spot a plane in the sky	60 mins. of activity
60 mins. of activity	Try an InPACT at Home activity Card	HAVE FUN! (Free Space)	Fly a kite	Read 20 minutes
Watch Read, Write, ROAR!	Spot a helicopter in the sky	Watch Math Mights	Watch InPACT at Home	Watch Live from the Opera House
Watch InPACT at Home	Read 20 minutes	Try Amelia Earhart's word find (pg. 12)	60 mins. of activity	Travel with Let's Go Luna (pg. 11)

Where Would You Go?

If you could travel anywhere with Luna, Carmen, Andy and Leo, where would you choose to go and why?

Find more game and activities at pbskidsforparents.org

Funded by:

Amelia Earhart's Travelling Word Find

F	T	P	L	A	N	E	E
U	T	N	S	N	R	M
N	X	K	K	A	A	T
D	F	L	Y	I	N	G
M	L	B	S	Z	I	M
H	P	I	L	O	T	W
P	A	C	K	V	N	E

Help Amelia find all the words related to her travels!

PLANE　　**FLYING**　　**PILOT**

SKY　　**PACK**　　**FUN**

Find more games and activities at pbskids.org/xavier

Produced by:

Sponsored by:

Based on Brad Meltzer and
Christopher Eliopoulos'
best-selling kids book series

Activity Cards

Cut out the cards. When you're feeling antsy, try following the directions for one of the exercises!

Blast-Off Lunges

INSTRUCTIONS

1. Get into a lunge position with left leg forward, hips underneath you, and right leg behind your right hip.
2. Slowly sink into a lunge, trying to get your knee to touch the ground.
3. Immediately "blast off" by hopping upwards and into next lunge position with right leg forward and left leg behind.
4. If needed, instead of jumping into the next lunge position, jump with feet together and then bounce into lunge position.
5. Repeat as many rounds as possible.

Side Leg Lifts

INSTRUCTIONS

1. Start by laying on your side with your legs stacked on top of each other.
2. Slowly raise your top leg up towards the sky and then back down.
3. Complete 10 repetitions and then switch legs.
4. Complete 3 sets per leg.
5. For added challenge, tape a bag of water to the top leg for some added weight!

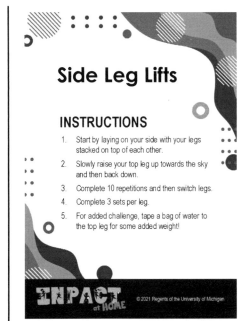

Tap Backs

INSTRUCTIONS

1. Stand up tall and proud with your feet together and hands on your hips.
2. Take your right foot and tap it right behind you, then place back to starting position.
3. Take your left foot and tap it right behind you, then place back to starting position.
4. Repeat as fast as can to get 100 tapbacks (50 on each leg).

Ski Jumps

INSTRUCTIONS

1. Start by standing tall with your feet shoulder width apart.
2. Using only your right foot, jump to the left about 2-3 feet and land on your left foot.
3. Gather yourself and then using only your left foot, jump to the right 2-3 feet and land on your right foot.
4. Repeat this as many times as you can for 30 seconds.

Bonus: After each time you jump, touch the ground with the same hand as the side you landed on. Ex: Land on your left foot, touch the ground with your left hand.

Cereal Bowl

INSTRUCTIONS

1. Lay flat on your back with feet together.
2. Bring your knees together and raise both legs up so that your feet are facing the ceiling.
3. In slow motion, stir the imaginary bowl of cereal with feet and keep hands under your bottom.
4. Repeat 30 times.

Lay Down Hip Stretch

INSTRUCTIONS

1. Start by sitting at the edge of a bed in a relaxed position with your feet hanging off.
2. Lay back, and pull your right knee towards your chest while keeping your left leg hanging off of the bed.
3. Pull your knee until you feel a stretch in your left hip and hold for 10-15 seconds.
4. Relax, switch legs, and then repeat 2-3 times per leg.

Aligator Breath

INSTRUCTIONS

1. Stand with legs hip-width apart.
2. Spread arms out wide and inhale as you reach outward.
3. When you exhale, clap your hands together as many times as possible like baby alligator jaws.

Cloud Watching

INSTRUCTIONS

1. Find a day where there are a lot of clouds in the sky.
2. Lay down on your back on the ground or in the grass and look up into the sky.
3. Watch and admire all the different clouds. Look at the different shapes they make, how fast/slow they're moving, and where they are moving to!

This page was left blank to cut out the
activity on the other side.

Paper Airplane

1. **Fold paper in half the long way and reopen.**

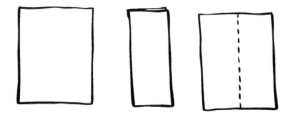

2. **Fold the top two corners into the center spine of the paper.**

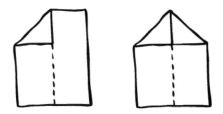

3. **Refold lengthwise and rotate the paper to lay on the table like this:**

4. **Fold the top left corner down to lay parallel to the bottom spine. Repeat this step on the other side.**

5. **Turn the paper over and repeat the last two steps. Your airplane should look like this!**

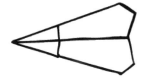

6. **Now, try to fly it to the moon! How far can you make the airplane fly?**

For more games and activities, visit pbskidsforparents.org

Produced by:

WIND DANCER
FILMS

Funded by:

Corporation for Public Broadcasting

The contents of this document were developed under a cooperative agreement (PR/Award No. U295A150003, CFDA No. 84.295A) from the U.S. Department of Education. However, these contents do not necessarily represent the policy of the Department of Education, and you should not assume endorsement by the Federal Government. © 2018 Jet Propulsion, LLC. Ready Jet Go! and the Ready Jet Go! logo are registered trademarks of Jet Propulsion, LLC. The PBS KIDS logo and PBS KIDS ® PBS. Used with permission. Corporate Funding of Ready Jet Go! is brought to you by ABCmouse.com. Made available by the Corporation for Public Broadcasting, a private corporation funded by the American people.

Sponsored by:
ABCmouse.com®

Pollinators

EXPLORE: Be a Bat!

Students model how bats and other pollinators help plants by spreading pollen from flower to flower.

Materials:

- **Cups**
- **Pompoms or cotton balls**
- **Colored sugar or confetti**
  Add food coloring to sugar or make confetti with a hole punch and tissue paper.
- **Kid-friendly tweezers**
- **60 second timer**

"FLOWERS"

Instructions:

1. Coat the inside of several cups, each with a different color of sugar. These are your flowers.

2. Fill the cups halfway with small pompoms (nectar) that match the color of the sugar in that cup and place around the room.

3. Give each student a pair of kid-friendly tweezers to be their pollinator "nose" and their own cup where they can collect pompoms.

4. Start a timer for 60 seconds. Students need to collect as many different colored pompoms as they can by visiting all the cups around the room. Have each "pollinator" pick up the pom-poms one at a time with their tweezers, lift them out of the flowers, and drop them in their own cups.

5. After 60 seconds, check the flower cups to see if any pollen (sugar) traveled from one flower to another. If the colors got mixed together, that means the flowers were pollinated.

TWEEZER "NOSE"

it's Storytime CHALLENGE

Bernoulli's Pressure Challenge

- Strip of Paper
- Ping Pong Ball
- Bendable Straw
- Round Cheese Puff
- Thin Garbage Bag
- Aluminum Cans
- String
- Clean Funnel
- Hair Dryer

My Design Ideas:

How could I improve on my design for next time?

DID YOU KNOW?

Bernoulli's principle explains the reason why airplanes are able to fly.

Between 1725 and 1749 alone, Daniel Bernoulli received 10 prizes from the Paris Academy of Sciences.

POWER UP WORDS

- Aviation
- Flight Path
- Cargo

CAREER LIFTOFF

- Pilot
- Air Traffic Controller
- Aerospace Engineer
- Avionics Technicians

Learning Standards: 3rd grade; Engineering Design
3-5-ETS1-1 Define a simple design problem reflecting a need or a want that includes specified criteria for success and constraints on materials, time, or cost.
3-5-ETS1-2 Generate and compare multiple possible solutions to a problem based on how well each is likely to meet the criteria and constraints of the problem.
3-5-ETS1-3 Plan and carry out fair tests in which variables are controlled and failure points are considered to identify aspects of a model or prototype that can be improved.

CITY OPERA HOUSE

TCAPS — Traverse City Area Public Schools — Great Community, Great Schools

Michigan LEARNING CHANNEL — A PUBLIC MEDIA PARTNERSHIP

LIVE from the OPERA HOUSE it's Storytime

ACTIVITY GUIDE

Episode 202: Up in the sky! and A Narrative Story

Scan below to watch lesson

Read It

Think of ideas for a narrative story about a time when the daytime or nighttime sky was an important part of the story. Write your ideas on the lines below.

1._____

2._____

3._____

4._____

5._____

Write It

Reread the list of topics that you made above. Before choosing a topic to write about, use the questions below to help you decide which topic is the best fit for your story. Cross out the topics that don't meet your needs.

1. Which topics have important parts that are related to the daytime or nighttime sky?
2. Which topics have something to do with the sky and why it was that way during that time of year?
3. Which topics do I remember well enough to write a story about? Do I remember who was there, how I felt, what it looked like? Will the sky be an important part of the story?
4. Which story am I excited to write about that will help me think about the importance of the daytime or nighttime sky? Who will I share it with?

ACTIVITY GUIDE

Episode 201: Earth's Landforms and -tch words
Book: *Earth's Landforms and Bodies of Water* by Natalie Hyde

Scan below to watch lesson

Phonics Skills

Landforms are natural features on the Earth's surface. Look at the numbers on the picture below. Write a word from the *Words to Know* box to label each number with the correct landform.

1. _____   2. _____

3. _____   4. _____

🔍 What types of landforms do you have where you live?

Words to Know

- **mountain** - a high raised landform that has sloping sides that form a peak.
- **hill** - a high raised landform that is smaller than a mountain with a rounded top.
- **valley** - an area found between raised landforms such as mountains or hills.
- **plains** - large. flat areas of land usually covered in grasses.

ACTIVITY GUIDE

Episode 202: More Prefixes and Saving the Trout
Book: *Underwater Adventures with Louis and Louise* by Stephen Schram

Scan below to watch lesson

Phonics Skills

Read the passage out loud. Underline the words with the **prefix** fore- and trans-.

Did you know the Blackpoll Warbler bird weighs less than a pencil? And yet it takes a transoceanic trip every winter! Before using a GPS, scientists didn't foresee this tiny bird flying across the ocean. They were surprised! Scientists think the foremost goal of the Warbler is to migrate quickly.

Words to Know

A **prefix** is a word part added to the beginning of a word that changes the meaning of the word.

The prefix **trans-** means "across" or "beyond".

The prefix **fore-** means "before" or "in front of".

🔍 Look for the trans- and fore- prefixes in your own reading.

Write It

Break each word into syllables and write the word parts in the blanks provided.

word	syllables		meaning
foresee	fore	see	to see before it happens
forewarn			to warn before something happens
foremost			most important
transoceanic			to go across the ocean
transfix			to make something motionless
transplant			to move something from one place to another

10 Frame Shake!

Shake a cup with 10 two-sided counters and dump it out. Count how many of each color you have and record it in the number sentence and number bond. Keep going until you have all 9 combinations for 10.

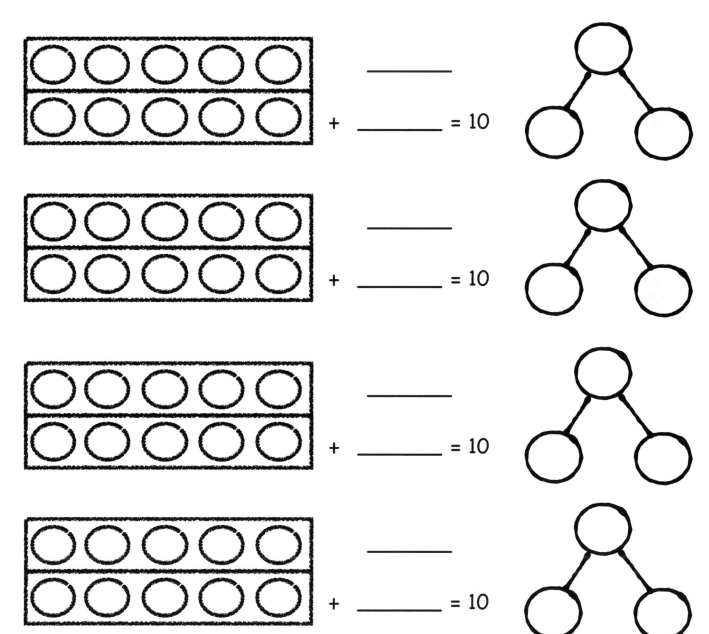

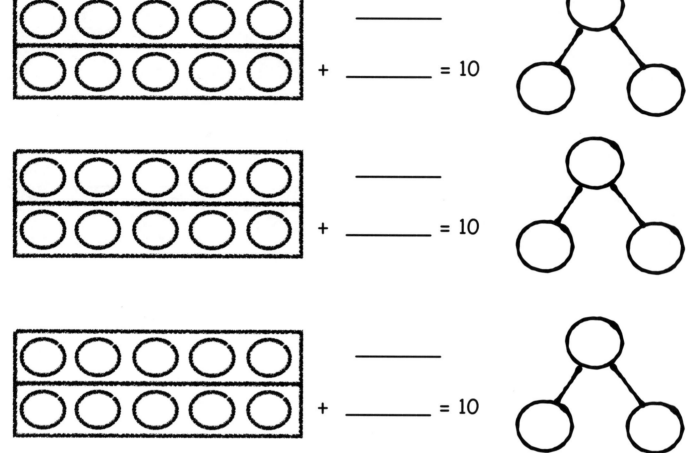

_____

+ _____ = 10

_____

+ _____ = 10

_____

+ _____ = 10

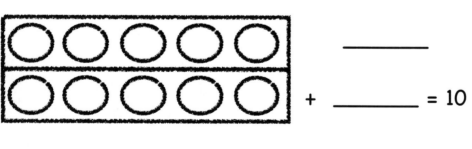

_____

+ _____ = 10

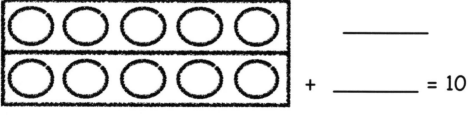

_____

+ _____ = 10

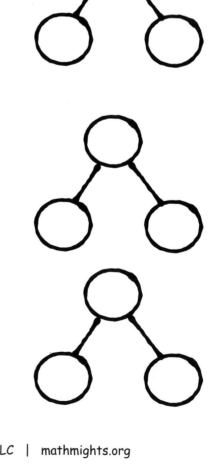

5 Way Callenge

Write the number 5 ways.

356	Only Tens and Ones
A Base Ten Diagram	Word Form
Compose a Different Way	Expanded Form

Reading and Writing Fractions

Directions: Label each part of the pictures and practice reading the fraction.

Example:

$\frac{1}{4}$ $\frac{1}{4}$
$\frac{1}{4}$ $\frac{1}{4}$

Practice reading: one fourth

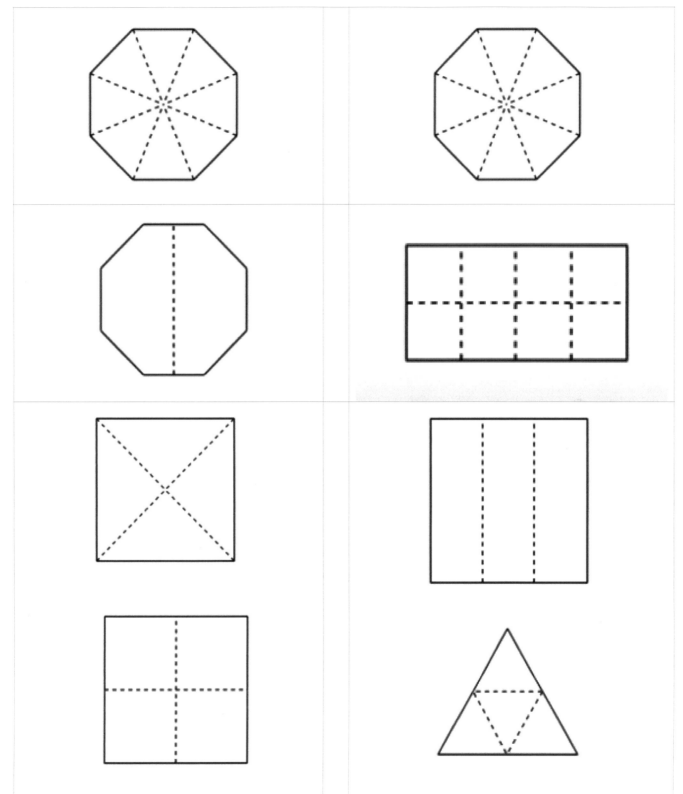

Week 2: Under Water

June 27 – July 3

Dive deep into oceans, rivers, and our own Great Lakes to discover what it takes to live beneath the waves.

Use the sheet below to mark off this week's activities as you complete them. See if you can get a BINGO!

Playlists this week: www.michiganlearning.org/underwater

Make a pond viewer (pg. 29)	60 mins. of activity	Read 20 minutes	Draw a deep sea fish (pg. 28)	Watch Read, Write, ROAR!
Read 20 minutes	Watch Math Mights	Go fishing	Watch Live from the Opera House	60 mins. of activity
60 mins. of activity	Try the Glorious Great Lakes Challenge	HAVE FUN! (Free Space)	Go swimming	Read 20 minutes
Watch Read, Write, ROAR!	Watch an ice cube change over time (pg. 31)	Watch Math Mights	Watch InPACT at Home	Watch Wimee's Words
Watch InPACT at Home	Read 20 minutes	Start a paper tracker (pg. 32)	60 mins. of activity	Tidy up the kelp forest! (pg. 27)

Tidy up the Kelp Forest!

Instructions: Tyke the Pacific Harbor Seal has hidden items that don't belong in the ocean. Can you help Tidy the Garibaldi Fish clean up? Circle the eight items that don't belong.

Reeftown Ranger Tip:

Never throw trash in the street. Rain can wash it down the storm drain and into rivers and streams. All rivers lead to the ocean!

Find more games and activities at pbskidsforparents.org

Can you draw a deep sea fish with BIG EYES, a BIG MOUTH, and LONG TEETH?

Fin Fact!

Creatures that live in the deep typically have large mouths, long teeth and hinged jaws to eat large quantities of scarce food. Many deep sea creatures also have very large eyes to capture scarce light.

FUNDING PROVIDED BY:

A POND WITH A VIEW

DIFFICULTY: EASY

While there is action all around a pond, what do you think is happening *in* the water? Ponds are filled with animal and plant life that have special qualities that help them spend all or most of their lives underwater. Make this pond viewer to bring on your next pond exploration!

MATERIALS

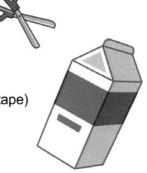

- One-half gallon milk carton
- Scissors
- Waterproof, strong tape (e.g. duct tape) or a sturdy rubber band
- Heavy, clear plastic wrap

LET'S MAKE A POND VIEWER!

1. Have an adult cut off the very top of the milk carton and the very bottom to create a rectangular tube.

2. Tear off a sheet of plastic wrap and place it over one of the open ends. Fold down the plastic wrap… make sure wrap is smooth and tight for clear viewing.

3. Using the tape or the rubber band, secure the plastic wrap in place. Keep the plastic wrap as tight as possible so you have a flat viewing surface.

pbskids.org/naturecat

POND VIEWING TIPS

1. Splashing and stirring up mud will make it difficult to see into the pond. Be as still as possible when using your viewer.

2. Despite what NatureCat says, it is noble and fun to get wet! If the shoreline is murky, slowly wade out to your knees before using your viewer where it may be less murky.

3. Other ways to view: on a dock, over the side of a canoe, or in a stream, lake or tide pool!

LET'S TAKE A CLOSER LOOK

Describe a plant or animal that you see. Draw a picture of it, and ask an adult to help you identify and label your picture.

pbskids.org/naturecat

Ice Cubes and Water: Now and Later

Name _____

Instructions:

1. Fill one plastic, clear cup with water and a second plastic, clear cup with ice.
2. Find a piece of chalk, a pencil, and take the two cups and this paper and go outside.
3. Pour a small amount of water on the ground. Outline the water puddle with chalk. In the first column, draw what you notice about the water.
4. Next, place one of your ice cubes on the ground and outline it with chalk. Leave one ice cube in a clear cup. After 30-minutes, in the second column, draw what you observe about the ice.
5. When another 30-minutes pass, write or draw a question you are interested in.

During my investigation I noticed this about the water...

When I first poured the water on the ground, the water looked like this...	After 30-minutes, the water I poured looked like this...

I observed this about the ice...

When I first placed the ice on the ground, the ice looked like this...	After 30-minutes, the ice looked like this..

What do you notice about how liquid water changed? _____

_____

_____

What do you notice about how solid water (ice) changed? _____

_____

_____

A question I still wonder about is... _____

_____

I made the connection in my mind when I observed the water and ice that... _____

_____

Find more games and activities at pbskidsforparents.org

Sponsored by:

The contents of this document were developed under a cooperative agreement (PR/Award No. U295A150003, CFDA No. 84.295A) from the U.S. Department of Education. However, these contents do not necessarily represent the policy of the Department of Education, and you should not assume endorsement by the Federal Government. © 2021 Jet Propulsion, LLC. Ready Jet Go! and the Ready Jet Go! logo are registered trademarks of Jet Propulsion, LLC. The PBS KIDS logo and PBS KIDS ® PBS. Used with permission. Corporate Funding is provided by ABCmouse.com. Made available by the Corporation for Public Broadcasting, a private corporation funded by the American people.

PAPER TRACKER RASTREADOR DE PAPEL

The paper you use at home comes from trees. Find out how much paper you use in a month.

1. Every time you go to throw away or recycle a piece of paper or cardboard, put it aside in a bag or box instead.

2. Then recycle any clean paper and compost or throw away any food-stained paper

3. Repeat this every week for a month.

4. At the end of the month, add up the number of pounds of paper you threw away each week. Put the total in the box in the chart below.

El papel que usas en casa viene de los árboles. Averigua cuánto papel utilizas en un mes.

1. Cada vez que vayas a tirar o reciclar un trozo de papel o cartón, guárdalo en una bolsa o caja.

2. Luego recicla el papel limpio y desecha el papel manchado de comida.

3. Repite esto cada semana durante un mes.

4. Al final del mes, suma la cantidad de libras de papel que desechaste cada semana. Pon el total en el cuadro de la tabla a continuación.

pounds of paper
libras de papel

	pounds of paper / libras de papel
Week 1 / Semana 1	
Week 2 / Semana 2	
Week 3 / Semana 3	
Week 4 / Semana 4	
TOTAL	

pounds of paper
libras de papel

If 100 people all used this much paper each month, how much paper would they use all together?

Si 100 personas usaran esta cantidad de papel cada mes, ¿cuánto papel usarían todos juntos?

100 people
100 personas
x [ ] total pounds of paper per person / total de libras de papel por persona = [ ] pounds of paper / libras de papel

To find out how many trees it takes to make that much paper, use a calculator to multiply the total by .012.

Para saber cuántos árboles se necesitan para hacer esa cantidad de papel, utiliza una calculadora para multiplicar el total por 0.012.

[ ] pounds of paper / libras de papel x **.012** trees per pound / árboles por libra = [ ] trees / árboles

Write down one thing you can do at home to use less paper
Escribe una cosa que puedas hacer en casa para utilizar menos papel

it's Storytime CHALLENGE

Glorious Great Lakes

REUSE Toolbox

What other materials could you find and use?

- Cardboard
- Glue
- Scissors
- Colored Paper
- Paper Towels
- Shaving Cream
- Beach Rocks

My Design Ideas:

POWER UP WORDS

- Peninsula
- Lake
- Fresh Water

How could I improve on my design for next time?

DID YOU KNOW

The five Great Lakes - Superior, Huron, Michigan, Erie and Ontario - span a total surface area of 94,600 square miles, making them the largest freshwater system in the world. More than 20% of the world's freshwater is in the Great Lakes!

CAREER LIFTOFF

- Coast Guard
- Environmental Engineer
- Conservationist
- National Park Service

Learning Standards: 2nd grade

Develop a model to represent the shapes and kinds of land and bodies of water in an area.

2-ESS2-2 MI Develop a model to represent the state of Michigan and the Great Lakes, or a more local land area and water body.

ACTIVITY GUIDE

Episode 204: Day and Night and Fun with -sh-, -th-, and -ch-

Scan below to watch lesson

Read It

Read the following poem out loud with someone you live with. Underline the words with the **sc** and **sk** blends.

Look up at the sky,
Do you see the clouds skip?
Sketch the night sky,
Do the stars seem to flip?
I have my book in hand to sketch all that I see,
Scoop up your markers or crayons and try to join me!

By Shernita Rodgers

Read It

Some words have two consonants that blend together at the beginning of words but still produce their own sounds. You will find this in the **s** blends **sc** and **sk**.

The s and c blend together to say /sc/.

The s and k blend together to say /sk/.

Sound out the words below. Then blend the sc and sk sounds together.

s c a n	scan
s k i p	skip

Write It

Think about the story that you have been writing. What might be a good **lead sentence** to hook your readers? Remember to include the four w's.

Who _____ Where _____ What _____

When _____

_____

_____

_____

ACTIVITY GUIDE

Episode 204: Earthquakes, Eruptions and "thr" words
Book: *Earthquakes, Eruptions, and Other Events that Change Earth* by Natalie Hyde

Scan below to watch lesson

Write It

Thr- is a blend that usually comes at the beginning of a word. It makes the /thr/ sound like in **thr**ob. Use a **thr-** word from the word box to complete each sentence.

through	throw	throat	thrill	three	thread	throne

1. To pitch a ball, you _____ it.

2. This is the number that comes next in this sequence. one, two ,_____.

3. A king has a special chair that he sits in. It's called a _____.

4. An airplane can fly _____ a cloud.

5. Someone who is sewing is most likely going to use a needle and _____ to stitch the sweater up.

6. It was such a _____ to ride on that big roller coaster.

7. I was nervous and had to clear my _____, before I began my speech.

Draw It

Alliteration is when two or more words close together in a group of words all start with the same letter or sound. Read the following sentence out loud. Draw a picture to go with the sentence.

Shelly shows sheep how to shine shoes.

ACTIVITY GUIDE

Episode 203: Suffixes and Saving the Salmon
Book: *Swimming Salmon* by Kathleen Martin-James

Scan below to watch lesson

Phonics Skills

Read the paragraph out loud. Circle the words with the -ous and -en suffixes.

When visiting a lake, you might see a Ring-billed Gull. Although these birds eat fish and insects, you should tighten your grip on your sandwich. These adventurous gulls might feast on your leftovers! Cleaning up your snacks encourages gulls to eat their natural foods.

Try It

A **suffix** is a word part added to the end of a word to change a word and its meaning.

-ous
full of, having

-en
to cause to be or have

We often drop the -e on base words when we add suffixes that start with vowels.

Write It

Combine each base word with the given suffix. Write the new word in the space provided and read each definition. Try using the new words in a sentence, and share them with a family member.

base word	suffix	new word	meaning
danger	ous		full of danger
fame	ous		full of fame
fright	en		to cause to be afraid
sharp	en		to cause to become sharp

Add & Subtract with Teen Numbers with Value Pak

Equation	Solve by drawing base ten blocks or model in a double ten frame
$13 = 10 + \square$	
$10 + 6 = \square$	
$17 = \square + 7$	
$10 + \square = 15$	
$2 = 10 - \square$	
$14 - 10 = \square$	
$\square = 18 - 10$	

Plot and Compare

Directions: Plot the numbers given on the number line and use <, >, or = to compare the two numbers (example: 3 < 13).

1.

600	610	620	630	640	650	660	670	680	690	700

Plot: **681, 618**

Compare (use <, >, or =) : _____ ____ _____

2.

300	310	320	330	340	350	360	370	380	390

Plot: **315, 366**

Compare (use <, >, or =) : _____ ____ _____

3.

400	500	600

Plot: **560, 460**

Compare (use <, >, or =) : _____ ____ _____

Math Mights 2nd Grade #303 | © Strategic Intervention Solutions, LLC | mathmights.org

Fraction Match Up

Directions: Cut out all the cards. Scatter the cards face down in two piles, one with the fraction cards and one with the shape cards. 2 players take turns flipping over one card from each pile, trying to make a match. If you make a match, keep the pair next to you. If you don't make a match, flip both cards over and it's the other player's turn. The player with the most matching pairs wins!

$\dfrac{5}{6}$	$\dfrac{1}{4}$	$\dfrac{7}{8}$
$\dfrac{3}{8}$	$\dfrac{2}{6}$	$\dfrac{1}{2}$

Week 3: Heroes

Celebrate our nation's birthday and the people we call heroes, whether they are veterans, everyday helpers, or the kind who wear capes.

Use the sheet below to mark off this week's activities as you complete them. See if you can get a BINGO!

Playlists this week: www.michiganlearning.org/heroes

Design a gadget (pg. 43)	60 mins. of activity	Read 20 minutes	Make bubble mix (pg. 44)	Watch Read, Write, ROAR!
Read 20 minutes	Watch Math Mights	Spot a mail truck outside	Do a good deed	60 mins. of activity
60 mins. of activity	Try the Cyberchase planting puzzle	HAVE FUN! (Free Space)	Watch Meet the Helpers	Read 20 minutes
Watch Read, Write, ROAR!	Do a good deed	Watch Math Mights	Watch InPACT at Home	Make superhero wrist cuffs (pg. 41)
Watch InPACT at Home	Read 20 minutes	Try a new food	60 mins. of activity	Spot a fire truck outside

Recycled Superhero Wrist Cuffs

AJ Gadgets uses his Superpowers of Science to engineer cool new gadgets from recycled materials. Join Sparks' Crew by making your own HERO ELEMENTARY superhero wrist cuffs from empty toilet paper rolls.

Directions:

1. Find two empty toilet paper rolls and make a cut down the length of each one so that you can slip one over each wrist.

2. Decorate your superhero wrist cuffs! You can use paint, markers, glitter, yarn, fabric or your favorite art supplies.

3. Color and cut out the images below and affix one to each wrist cuff. Can you find other recycled materials from around your house to add to your cuff?

4. Wear your wrist cuffs and remember you can be a superhero by being kind and helping others!

AJ Gadgets

For more games and activities, visit pbskidsforparents.org

Funded by:

©2021 Twin Cities Public Television, Inc. All rights reserved. Hero Elementary characters, artwork, and underlying materials are trademarks and copyrights of Twin Cities Public Television, Inc. The PBS KIDS wordmark and the PBS KIDS Logo are registered trademarks of Public Broadcasting Service. Used with permission.

The contents of this program were developed under a grant from the U.S. Department of Education (PR U295A150012). However, those contents do not necessarily represent the policy of the Department of Education, and you should not assume endorsement by the Federal Government. Made available by the Corporation for Public Broadcasting, a private sorporation funded by the American people.

Funding for Hero Elementary is provided by a Ready To Learn grant from the U. S. Department of Education. Additional funding made possible by ABCmouse.com and Target.

This page was left blank to cut out the
activity on the other side.

Gadget Gurus

Create a gadget! AJ Gadgets makes super tools from everyday items. You can too! Create a gadget from recyclables. Think about AJ's greatest gadgets: Arm-O-Matic, Rope Launcher, Twigcam, Dragonfly Drone, Launcher, Lacer Racer, Tooth Brushing Gadget, Night Vision Goggles. Next, take some time to think about what you would like to build. Draw your ideas below. Then, gather objects to complete your design! Be sure to ask a grownup for help if you need it.

What you need:

- **Pencil and eraser Recyclables**:
- cardboard boxes, plastic bottles, tin cans, newspapers/magazines, old toys, or other old objects (don't use if there are sharp edges)

- **Joiners**: tape, glue, string, wire, pipe cleaners
- **Decorators**: paint, crayons, markers, stickers, and other craft supplies
- **Cutters**: scissors, hole punchers, etc. Be sure to use a grownup helper!

For more games and activities, visit pbskids.org/heroelementary

The contents of this program were developed under a grant from the U.S. Department of Education (PR U295A150012). However, those contents do not necessarily represent the policy of the Department of Education, and you should not assume endorsement by the Federal Government.

Funding for Hero Elementary is provided by a Ready To Learn grant from the U. S. Department of Education. Additional funding made possible by ABCmouse.com and Target.

Bubble Up!

Make a bubble mix at home for some outdoor fun!

What you need:
- 1/2 cup liquid dish soap
- 1/4 cup glycerin (from a pharmacy) or corn syrup (from a grocery)
- 2 cups water
- Bowl (or bucket)
- Spoon or chopstick

What to do:
Pour water, dish soap, and glycerin (or corn syrup) into the bowl or bucket. Stir slowly to mix the liquids, but to keep bubbles from forming. Dip the wand you created (see below) into the mixture and blow bubbles!

Create a Wand!

What you need:
- Pipe cleaners
- Your choice of the following:
    - wire coat hanger
    - cookie cutters
    - old sandbox or beach toys
    - kitchen utensils (ask a parent first!)
    - fly swatter

What to do:
AJ Gadgets makes tools from everyday things and you can too! Create a bubble wand – small or supersized. The larger the bubble wand, the larger the bubbles!

A bubble wand has two parts:
1. A shape (circle or square) with a hole in the middle
2. A handle

Use pipe cleaners or wire to attach the two parts of the bubble wand.
Dip the wand into the bubble mixture you created (see above) and blow bubbles!

Find more games and activities at pbskids.org/heroelementary

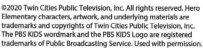

Funding for Hero Elementary is provided by a Ready To Learn grant from the U. S. Department of Education. Additional funding made possible by ABC Mouse.

My Summer Adventure

Dot, Dee and Dell love to explore and learn together. Write down or draw the places or things you'd like to explore this summer.

Find more games and activities at **pbskids.org**

it's Storytime CHALLENGE

Make Your Own Stethoscope

REUSE Toolbox
What other materials could you find and use?

- Duct tape
- Scissors
- Plastic Funnel
- Cardboard Tube
- Stopwatch or Clock

My Design Ideas:

How could I improve on my design for next time?

DID YOU KNOW?

Heroes are definitely in the medical field, but there are heroes everywhere! Police officers, teachers, scientists, firefighters, and soldiers are all heroes. And that's not all! Who in your community is a hero?

POWER UP WORDS

- Oxygen
- Exercise
- Heart Rate

CAREER LIFTOFF

- Physician
- Biomedical Engineer
- Nurse
- Physical Therapist
- Veterinarian

Learning Standards: 3rd grade

3-5-ETS1-3 Plan and carry out fair tests in which variables are controlled and failure points are considered to identify aspects of a model or prototype that can be improved.

CITY OPERA HOUSE

 TCAPS — Traverse City Area Public Schools — Great Community, Great Schools

 Michigan LEARNING CHANNEL — A PUBLIC MEDIA PARTNERSHIP

LIVE from the OPERA HOUSE it's Storytime

PLANTING PUZZLE

EL ROMPECABEZAS DE LA SIEMBRA

Flowers, like trees, help clean our air and make cities more beautiful. Help the CyberSquad plan out a community garden for a new Cyber Site, using these rules:

- Every **green flower** must be directly above, below, or to the side of a yellow flower

- Every **green flower** must also be directly above, below, or to the side of a **pink flower**

- **Pink flowers** can't be directly above, below, or to the side of another **pink flower**

Cut out the flowers on the last page. Use a crayon or marker to color in:

- ◾ **5 green flowers**
- ▨ **8 yellow flowers**
- ◾ **5 pink flowers**
- ◾ **7 blue flowers**

Use the grid on the next page to make your plan. Move the flowers around until you find a plan that follows all three rules above. Once you have them in place, glue them down to plant your garden.

Las flores, como los árboles, ayudan a limpiar nuestro aire y a embellecer las ciudades. Ayuda al CyberSquad a diseñar un jardín comunitario para un nuevo Cyber Site siguiendo estas reglas:

- Cada **flor verde** debe estar justo arriba, abajo o al lado de una flor amarilla

- Cada **flor verde** también debe estar justo arriba, abajo o al lado de una **flor rosa**

- **Las flores rosas** no pueden estar justo arriba, abajo o al lado de otra **flor rosa**

Recorta las flores que aparecen en la última página. Usa un crayón o marcador para colorear:

- ◾ **5 flores verdes**
- ▨ **8 flores amarillas**
- ◾ **5 flores rosas**
- ◾ **7 flores azules**

Usa la cuadrícula de la página siguiente para hacer tu plano. Cambia las flores de lugar hasta que encuentres un plano que siga las tres reglas anteriores. Una vez que las tengas en su lugar, pégalas para plantar tu jardín.

10

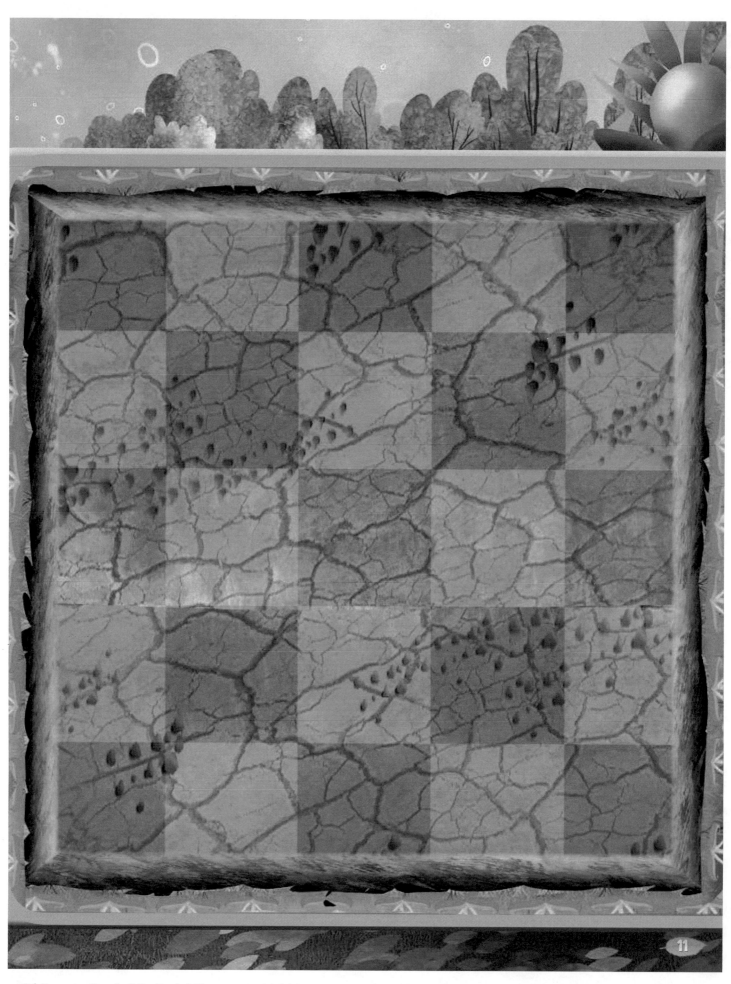

Use a crayon or marker to color in:
Utiliza un crayón o marcador para colorear:

⑤	⑧	⑤	⑦
GREEN	YELLOW	PINK	BLUE
VERDE	AMARILLO	ROSA	AZUL

PLANTING PUZZLE

EL ROMPECABEZAS
DE LA SIEMBRA

This page was left blank to cut out the
activity on the other side.

GROW YOUR OWN GARDEN

CULTIVA TU PROPIA HUERTA

Delicious, healthy vegetables don't just come from the store. You and your family can grow them from seeds at home! You don't need a big farm to grow vegetables. Even a small space can be home to a garden.

Use old newspapers to make a pot for planting seeds.

Materials:
- **masking tape**
- **newspaper**
- **seeds for vegetables or herbs**
- **potting soil**
- **a can or jar**

1. To make a newspaper pot:
   a. Tear two strips of newspaper the width of your hand (about 4" wide).
   b. Lay the two strips on top of each other.
   c. Place the can on its side at one end of the strip. Leave a little extra paper hanging off the bottom of the can.
   d. Roll the newspaper strips tightly around the can.
   e. When you get to the end, tape it down. Then fold up the extra newspaper over the bottom of the can and tape it down too.
   f. Pull the can out of the pot.
2. Fill the pot ½ full of soil.
3. Sprinkle some seeds on the soil. Cover the seeds with another layer of soil. Check the seed packet to see how much soil to add on top.
4. Place your pots on a plate or dish and put them by a window where they will get some light.
5. After the plant grows a few leaves, plant the whole pot in the ground or in a bigger pot. Over time, the newspaper will biodegrade (break down) in the soil.

Las verduras deliciosas y saludables no solo vienen de la tienda. ¡Tú y tu familia pueden cultivarlas a partir de semillas en casa! No necesitas una gran granja para cultivar verduras. Incluso un espacio pequeño puede albergar una huerta.

Usa periódicos viejos para hacer una maceta para plantar semillas.

Materiales:
- **cinta de enmascarar**
- **periódico**
- **semillas para verduras o hierbas**
- **tierra de macetas**
- **una lata o un frasco**

1. Para hacer una maceta de periódico, debes:
   a. Cortar dos tiras de papel de periódico del ancho de tu mano (alrededor de 4 pulgadas de ancho).
   b. Pon las dos tiras una encima de la otra.
   c. Pon la lata de lado en un extremo de la tira. Deja un poco de papel extra colgando del fondo de la lata.
   d. Enrolla las tiras de periódico con firmeza alrededor de la lata.
   e. Cuando llegues al final, ponle la cinta. Luego dobla el periódico extra sobre el fondo de la lata y pégalo con cinta también.
   f. Saca la lata de la maceta.
2. Llena la maceta hasta la mitad con tierra.
3. Esparce algunas semillas en la tierra. Cubre las semillas con otra capa de tierra. Revisa el paquete de semillas para ver cuánta tierra agregar en la parte superior.
4. Pon las macetas en un plato o una fuente y colócalas junto a una ventana donde reciban algo de luz.
5. Después de que crezcan algunas hojas, planta toda la maceta en la tierra o en una maceta más grande. Con el tiempo, el periódico se biodegradará (se descompondrá) en el suelo.

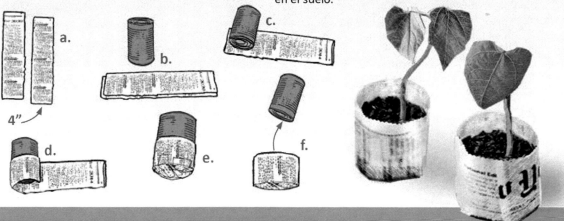

ACTIVITY GUIDE

Episode 206: Earth's Hemispheres and Character Dialogue

Scan below to watch lesson

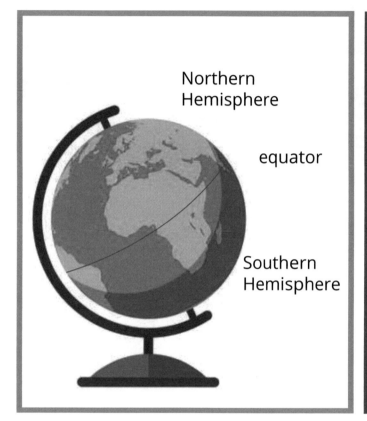

Northern Hemisphere

equator

Southern Hemisphere

Words to Know

equator - The imaginary line around the middle of the Earth

hemisphere - a half of a sphere or ball

opposite - completely different or located at another side or end

rotate - to move or spin from the center or axis in a circular motion

tilt - when an object is a little bit higher on one side than it is on the other side

Write It

Use the words from above to fill in the blanks.

The _____ separates the northern and southern

_____(s). We have day and night because the Earth

_____(s) on its axis. We have the seasons because the Earth is

_____(ed). If it is summer in the northern hemisphere then it is

winter in the southern hemisphere. That is because the northern and

southern hemispheres have _____ seasons.

ACTIVITY GUIDE

Episode 205: Earthquakes, Eruptions and Making Words
Book: *Earthquakes, Eruptions, and Other Events that Change Earth* by Natalie Hyde

Scan below to watch lesson

Foundational Skills

Read the words in the Word Bank. These are all processes that change the Earth's surface. Write a word from the Word Bank on the line that matches each picture and key word in the same row.

earthquake	volcano	tsunami	landslide

wave _____

slide _____

erupt _____

shake _____

ACTIVITY GUIDE

Episode 205: Prefixes and Saving the Salmon Part 1
Book: *Come Back, Salmon* by Molly Cone

Scan below to watch lesson

Read It

Read the paragraph out loud. Circle the words with the after- and under- prefixes.

Piping Plovers are hard to spot! These endangered, sandy-colored birds are almost invisible on the beach. It is easiest to see plovers when they sprint toward worms and insects that hide just underground. When plovers chase their afternoon snack, you might see their white underside and orange legs.

Foundational Skills

A **prefix** is a word part added to the beginning of a word to change a word and its meaning.

after-
later or after

under-
below or less

Try It

Combine each base word with the given prefix. Write the new word in the space provided and read each definition. Try using the new words in a sentence, and share them with a family member.

base word	prefix	new word	meaning
effect	after-		result that happens after some time has passed
eat	over-		eat less than you should
thought	after-		something you think about later
ground	under-		below ground

Make a 10 With D.C.

Directions: Use the ten frames to make 10. Solve the addition problem.

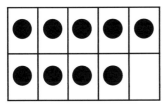

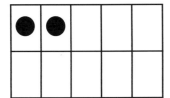

____ + ____ = ____

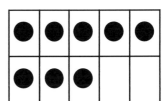

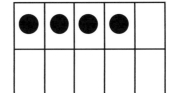

____ + ____ = ____

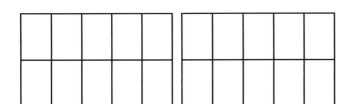

7 + 5 = ☐

____ + ____ = ____

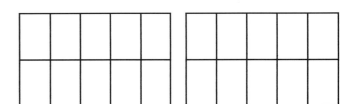

9 + 8 = ☐

____ + ____ = ____

Which is Greater?

Materials:
- spinner (poke a paperclip through the template to the right)
- place value board (one for each partner)

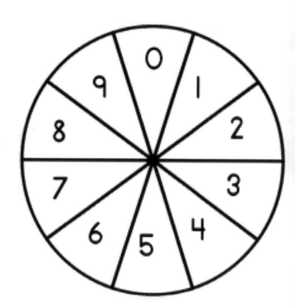

Directions:
1. Work with a partner to try to make the greatest 3-digit number you can.
2. Player 1 spins. Player 1 decides if the number should go in the ones, tens, or hundreds place to make the largest 3-digit number. (ex: I rolled a 2 and I think it should go in the ones place because it is a low number. In the hundreds place, it would only be 200.) Use the place value board to build your number.
3. Player 2 repeats step 2. Continue taking turns spinning until both players have built their 3-digit number. Record your numbers on the chart below.
4. Work with your partner to compare the 2 numbers and fill in <, >, =. The player with the greater number wins! Play 5 rounds and the best out of 5 wins!

Round	Player 1	Symbol < > =	Player 2	Winner
1				
2				
3				
4				
5				

Place Value Boards

hundreds	tens	ones

hundreds	tens	ones

Locate the Fraction

Directions: Partition each number line. Locate and label each fraction.

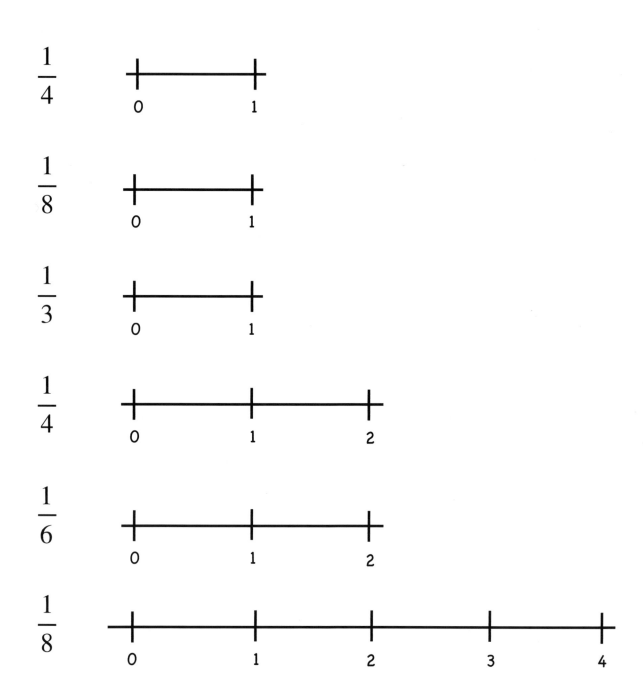

Week 4: Creatures July 11-17

From the prehistoric to the present, learn about the fascinating features of creatures near and far.

Use the sheet below to mark off this week's activities as you complete them. See if you can get a BINGO!

Playlists this week: www.michiganlearning.org/creatures

Invent a creepy cool creature (62)	60 mins. of activity	Read 20 minutes	Catch a firefly	Watch Read, Write, ROAR!
Read 20 minutes	Watch Math Mights	Make tracks with clay (pg. 63)	Make bird observations (pg. 64)	60 mins. of activity
60 mins. of activity	Make a Rube Goldberg Machine	HAVE FUN! (Free Space)	Track the weather	Read 20 minutes
Watch Read, Write, ROAR!	Go fishing	Watch Math Mights	Watch InPACT at Home	Make a leftover recipe (pg. 66)
Watch InPACT at Home	Read 20 minutes	Write a creature adventure (pg. 61)	60 mins. of activity	Move like a dinosaur (pg. 60)

Move Like a Dinosaur

Instructions: Can you move like a dinosaur? Here's a list of movements to get you and your child started! To play, have your child stand at one end of the room and move towards you using one of the prompts below.

 WALK like a Theropod
(a bipedal dinosaur that walked on two legs)

 MOVE like a Brachiosaurus
(a quadrupedal dinosaur that walked on all fours)

 SPRINT like an Ornithomimus
(a dinosaur with long thin legs for sprinting or running really fast)

 GLIDE like a Microraptor
(a small bird-like dinosaur that could move smoothly through the air)

 SLITHER like a Sanajeh
(a prehistoric snake that slithered or slid around on its belly)

 STOMP like a T. rex!
(a powerful dinosaur who walked around with loud, heavy steps)

 DIVE like a Hesperonis
(a dinosaur that was good at diving deep underwater for fish)

 FLY like a Pteranodon
(like Tiny, Shiny, and Don, Pteranodons could fly through the air very easily)

 SWIM backwards like a Michelinoceras
(a squid-like creature who lived in the ocean and swam backwards)

 HOOT like a Corythosaurus
(a dinosaur with a large crest on top of its head that
made a hooting sound like a horn)

Funded by:

PBS KIDS and the PBS KIDS Logo are registered trademarks of Public Broadcasting Service. Used with permission. Dinosaur Train TM & © 2020 The Jim Henson Company. All Rights Reserved. Corporate funding is provided by ABCmouse.com and Kiddie Academy®.

My Creature Adventure

Instructions: It's time to write a creature adventure! To get started, choose a creature and a setting (where the adventure takes place). Then, decide on the plot (what happens to the creature in the setting). Use the space below to begin the story.

Corporate Funding of Wild Kratts is provided by
ADVENTURE ACADEMY

Invent A Creepy Cool Creature

Think about what features make a creature creepy. Draw the creepiest creature you can invent, then make a cool Creature Power® suit for Martin to wear.

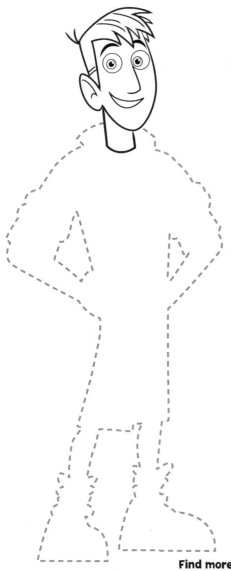

MAKIN' TRACKS WITH PLAY DOUGH!

DIFFICULTY: EASY

When you walk in wet sand, snow or mud, you leave behind a footprint. Animals do, too! We call those prints, "tracks." Next time you're exploring, look for tracks on the ground!

You can also make your own tracks to compare with friends, your pet, or one of the Nature Cat gang! Using play dough, make YOUR nature tracks to create an artistic masterpiece!

MATERIALS

- 🐾 Play dough
- 🐾 Rolling pin
- 🐾 Washable paint and paintbrush (optional)

CAPTURE YOUR TRACKS

1. Make two balls with your dough.

2. Roll out each dough ball on a flat surface until it is a little bit bigger than your foot.

3. Ready? Press your hand into one piece of the dough.

4. Now repeat with a foot (or a patient pet.)

5. Let it dry and add some color with paint!

Find more games and activities at **pbskidsforparents.org**

My Bird Observations

Look out a window and draw a bird that you see.
Tell someone else about the bird. Share what you notice — for example,
the colors of the feathers or the shape of its beak. What was it doing?

Find more games and activities at pbskidsforparents.org

 Corporation for Public Broadcasting

it's Storytime CHALLENGE

RUBE GOLDBERG MACHINE

REUSE Toolbox
What other materials could you find and use?

- Dominos or Blocks
- Ball
- Cardboard
- Duct Tape
- Balloon
- Push Pin

My Design Ideas:

How could I improve on my design for next time?

DID YOU KNOW?

Engineers usually design or build things. Some engineers also use their skills to solve technical problems. There are different types of engineers that design everything from computers and buildings to watches and websites.

POWER UP WORDS

- Slope
- Tension
- Gravity

CAREER LIFT-OFF

- Civil Engineer
- Mechanical Engineer
- Roller Coaster Engineer

Learning Standards: Kindergarten; Forces and Interactions: Pushes and Pulls

K-PS2-1 Plan and conduct an investigation to compare the effects of different strengths or different directions of pushes and pulls on the motion of an object.
K-PS2-2 Analyze data to determine if a design solution works as intended to change the speed or direction of an object with a push or a pull.

CITY OPERA HOUSE

TCAPS
Traverse City Area Public Schools
Great Community, Great Schools

Michigan LEARNING CHANNEL
A PUBLIC MEDIA PARTNERSHIP

LIVE from the OPERA HOUSE it's Storytime

LEFTOVER RECIPE CHALLENGE
DESAFÍO DE LA RECETA DE SOBRAS

Getting creative with leftovers helps waste less food! Can you help Jackie use her leftover foods to make an exciting new recipe? Pick three of the foods in Jackie's refrigerator below to combine into a new recipe. Draw your leftover creation on the recipe card on the next page. Be sure to add a name for your new dish!

¡Al usar las sobras de forma creativa, se desperdicia menos comida! ¿Puedes ayudar a Jackie a usar las sobras de comida para crear una receta nueva? Escoge tres alimentos del refrigerador de Jackie para combinarlos en una receta nueva. Dibuja lo que creaste en la tarjeta de recetas de la página siguiente. ¡No olvides escribir un nombre para tu plato nuevo!

Jackie's Leftovers / Las sobras de Jackie

- Carrots / Zanahorias
- Meatballs / Albóndigas
- Pasta / Pasta
- Chicken / Pollo
- Salad Greens / Ensalada de hojas verdes
- Apples / Manzanas
- Peppers / Pimientos
- Beans / Frijoles
- Cheese / Queso

4

MY NEW RECIPE
MI RECETA NUEVA

Try the same thing with leftovers at home! Make a list of the leftover food in your refrigerator, so that everyone in the family knows what you have. Challenge the whole family to use those leftovers to make new recipes. Don't forget to use "ugly" fruits and veggies too!"

¡Intenta hacer lo mismo con las sobras que tienes en casa! Haz una lista de las sobras de comida que tienes en tu refrigerador para que todos en tu familia sepan lo que hay. Desafía a toda la familia a usar esas sobras para crear recetas nuevas. "¡No olvides usar frutas y verduras que estén 'feas', también!"

Our Leftovers
Nuestras sobras

5

ACTIVITY GUIDE

Episode 208: Authors Share Writing

Scan below to watch lesson

Sort It

Blends are created when two consonant letters blend together at the beginning of words, but we can still hear each of their sounds.

Read the words in the word box below. Write each word under their correct S-blend.

star spend swam spin sweater storm swim spot stop

sp	sw	st

Read It

Read the following sentences out loud. Underline the words with the **sp**, **sw**, and **st** blends.

1. We looked for a spot on the crowded beach.
2. "A storm is coming!" said Matt.
3. Other people continued to swim.

Draw It

Draw a picture to match the sentence.

I wore a sweater during the winter storm.

Look out for words with the **sp**, **sw**, and **st** blends when reading your favorite books.

ACTIVITY GUIDE

Episode 208: Garbage vs. Recycling and Making Words
Book: *Garbage or Recycling?* by Deborah Chancellor and Diane Ewen

Scan below to watch lesson

Think About It

Read the following statements, Which are true and which are false?

It's impossible to recycle a soda pop can. _____

Over half of the garbage we throw out can be recycled. _____

Plastic garbage often ends up in the sea. _____

Words to Know

Recycling is when we take materials that we were going to throw away and put them through a process so they can be made into something else.

These symbols are found on **plastic** items that can be recycled.

Draw It

Look at each object. Decide if it can be recycled or if it should be thrown in the garbage. Draw a line from each object to where it belongs.

ACTIVITY GUIDE

Episode 207: Closed Syllables and Climate Challenges
Book: *Magic School Bus and the Climate Change Challenge* by Bruce Degen

Scan below to watch lesson

Read It

One strategy readers can use to read a word more accurately is to break it into syllables, or word parts.

Rules for Dividing Syllables
Every syllable has one vowel or vowel team.
-Place a dot under each vowel
-Underline any vowel teams,
-Divide between two consonants

Foundational Skills

A **syllable** is a word part that has one, and only one vowel sound. Sometimes a syllable will have more than one of these vowels, but they work together to make only one sound.

A **closed syllable** is a special kind of syllable. Closed syllables have ONLY one vowel that is followed by one or more consonants. Closed syllables USUALLY have vowels that make their short vowel sound.

Try It

Use the rules for dividing syllables above to break the words into word parts.

plastic

_____ _____

landfill

_____ _____

Michigan Learning Channel

Read, Write, ROAR!™ 3rd Grade Episode 207

Near Doubles with Abracus

Directions: Use the ten frames to solve the problems.

Ten Frame	Double	Double + 1
	7 + 7 = ___	7 + 8 = ___
	4 + 4 = ___	4 + 5 = ___
	8 + 8 = ___	8 + 9 = ___
	3 + 3 = ___	3 + 4 = ___
	6 + 6 = ___	6 + 7 = ___

Describe The Shape

Directions: Fill in the blanks. (Example: The rectangle is made up of 3 squares.)

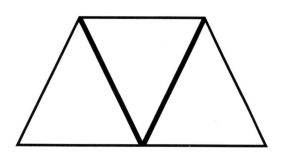

The _____ is made up
of ____ _____.

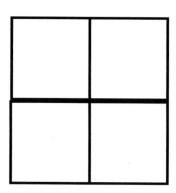

The _____ is made up
of ____ _____.

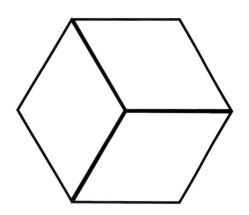

The _____ is made up
of ____ _____.

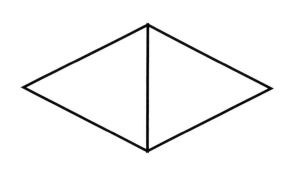

The _____ is made up
of ____ _____.

Math Mights 2nd Grade #310 | © Strategic Intervention Solutions, LLC | mathmights.org

Guess the Fraction

Directions: Guess which fraction is displayed with a dot on the number line. Label the fraction.

1.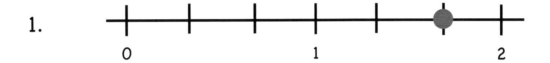

2.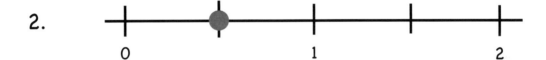

3.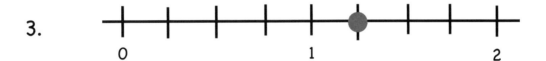

4.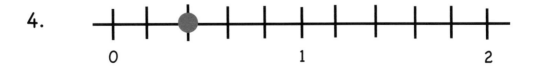

5.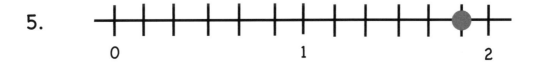

Week 5: Engineering

July 18-24

Meet the people who design bridges, cars, and video games and learn how to think like an engineer.

Use the sheet below to mark off this week's activities as you complete them. See if you can get a BINGO!

Playlists this week: www.michiganlearning.org/engineering

Watch Live from the Opera House	60 mins. of activity	Read 20 minutes	Act out Structures (pg. 79)	Watch Read, Write, ROAR!
Read 20 minutes	Watch Math Mights	Try the hexagon challenge! (pg. 75)	Travel the Food Miles Maze (pg. 80)	60 mins. of activity
60 mins. of activity	Watch Meet the Helpers	HAVE FUN! (Free Space)	Build and balance an object (pg. 78)	Read 20 minutes
Watch Read, Write, ROAR!	Ride a bike	Watch Math Mights	Watch InPACT at Home	Draw a family member's car
Watch InPACT at Home	Read 20 minutes	Try the Amazing Animals Challenge	60 mins. of activity	Watch ArchiTreks

The Hexagon Challenge

Use your Odd Squad agent skills to solve
The Hexagon Challenge. Print out the two pages.

1. Cut out all the shapes from the Shape Box.

2. On the next page, mix and match your shapes to make a hexagon.

3. Record how you did it by drawing the lines of each shape you used like in the example at the top.

4. Reuse your shapes again and again to make more hexagon patterns.
   Try to find **8 different** ways to make a hexagon.

Here's a hexagon made with 4 triangles and a rectangle.

Shape Box

Funded by:

ADVENTURE ACADEMY

ODD SQUAD© 2014 The Fred Rogers Company. All rights reserved. PBS KIDS and the PBS KIDS Logo are registered trademarks of Public Broadcasting Service. Used with permission. Corporate Funding of ODD SQUAD is brought to you by Adventure Academy. This document may be printed for personal, non-commercial purposes. Made available by the Corporation for Public Broadcasting, a private corporation funded by the American people.

 Corporation for Public Broadcasting

 Fred Rogers PRODUCTIONS

This page was left blank to cut out the
activity on the other side.

The Hexagon Challenge

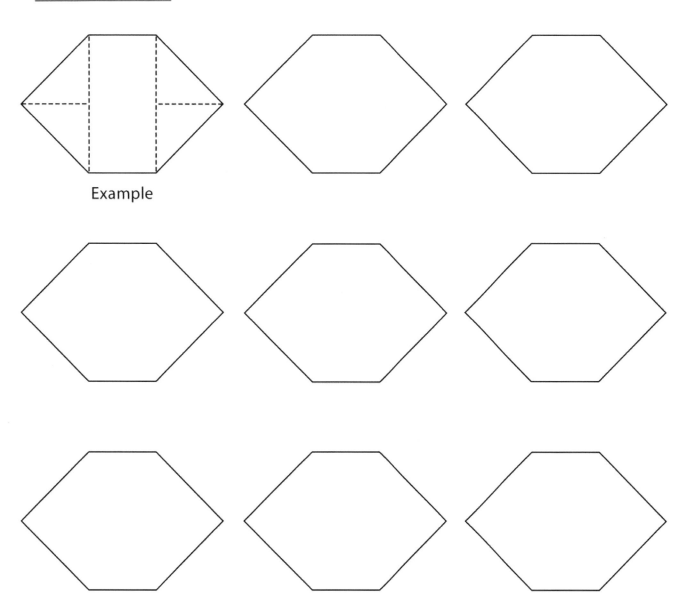

Example

When you are finished with the challenge, check out some possible solutions at www.fredrogers.org/odd-squad-hexagon-solution/

For more printables, go to pbskidsforparents.org

Balance Build

Students will explore symmetry and the properties of balance in this open-ended STEM challenge.

Materials: You can use anything that sparks imagination! Here are some examples.
- Paper
- Scissors
- Craft Sticks
- Beads
- Straws
- Clear Tape
- Masking Tape

Did you know?

Have you ever balanced a pencil or a ruler on your finger? If you have, you helped it reach a **state of equilibrium**. In order to balance an object, you have to find its **center of gravity**. In the case of your pencil, the center of gravity is the same as its midpoint. This is because pencils (and rulers) are **symmetrical** and have equal mass along its length.

Procedure:

1. First, select your materials to create a balancing object. We suggested a few above, but use what you have around your home and challenge your family members to engineer their own design!
2. Creating a symmetrical object, or something that is equal on both sides, will help you in your design process.
3. Once you are satisfied with your design, test it out! See if you can find your new inventions center of gravity to balance it on your finger.
4. What part of your design worked really well in order to achieve balance? Did you experience any failures during your build? What improvements could you make?

Keep Exploring:

Try creating an asymmetrical object that can balance on your finger, or try to create a build to balance on your nose!

1801 W. Saint Andrews Rd.
Midland, MI 48640

800.523.7649
midlandcenter.org

ArchiTREKS: Structures

Acting Out Structures

COLUMN

ARCH

COLUMN AND BEAM

DOME

TENSION

CANTILEVER

LOAD AND SUPPORT

VAULT / TUNNEL

COMPRESSION

FLYING BUTTRESSES

How does your house stay standing? Architects use structures like columns, beams, and arches to make buildings strong and be sure they last for many years. Grab a grown-up or a friend and try to make columns, beams, and arches with your body!

FOOD MILES MAZE

EL LABERINTO DE LAS MILLAS DE COMIDA

Sometimes food travels a long way to get from the farm to our table.

Draw a line to get the cherries from the farm to chef Digit in the maze below. Notice all the different types of transportation you use along the way. Add up the numbers from each type of transportation to see how many miles the cherries had to travel to get to Digit. Do it again and take a different path. Try to find the path with the lowest number of miles!

A veces la comida hace un gran recorrido para ir de la granja a nuestra mesa.

Dibuja una línea para llevar las cerezas desde la granja hasta el chef Digit a través del laberinto. Presta atención a los distintos tipos de transporte que usas en el camino. Suma los números de cada tipo de transporte para ver cuántas millas tuvieron que recorrer las cerezas para llegar a Digit. Luego, hazlo de nuevo, pero toma un camino diferente. ¡Intenta encontrar el camino que tenga menos millas!

100 MILES MILLAS

25 MILES MILLAS

15 MILES MILLAS

5 MILES MILLAS

35 MILES MILLAS

10 MILES MILLAS

Total Miles Travelled:
Total de millas recorridas:

6

it's Storytime CHALLENGE

Amazing Animals

REUSE Toolbox
What other materials could you find and use?

- Various Boxes
- Foam Blocks, Cubes & Balls
- Form Board
- Fun Fabrics
- Masking Tape
- Small Bag of Bird Seeds
- Pipe Cleaners
- Wiggly Eyes

My Design Ideas:

How could I improve on my design for next time?

DID YOU KNOW 2

Animals are truly amazing. Did you know that to hover, hummingbirds may beat their wings up to 200 times per second? Or that a jaguar can see in the dark six times better than a human?

POWER UP WORDS
- Adaptation
- Coexist
- Ecosystem

CAREER LIFTOFF
- Zoologist
- Wildlife Biologist
- Marine Rescue Officer
- Animal Shelter Technician

Learning Standards: 2nd Grade

2-LS2-2 Develop a simple model that mimics the function of an animal in dispersing seeds or pollinating plants.

CITY OPERA HOUSE

Michigan LEARNING CHANNEL
A PUBLIC MEDIA PARTNERSHIP

LIVE from the OPERA HOUSE it's Storytime

ACTIVITY GUIDE

Episode 210: Traveling Through Space

Scan below to watch lesson

High Frequency Words

High frequency words are words that show up a lot when we are reading and writing.

Or   When   What

Label It

Start at the bottom of the ladder. Say the word. Follow the instructions to change each word. Write the new word in the space provided.

Change the **nd** to a **mp**

Add a **t** after the **s**

Change the **h** to a **s**

Add an **n** before the **d**

Had

Words to Know

We build a **word ladder** by starting with a word and using what we know about letters and sounds to make a new word by changing one or two letters at a time. We start at the bottom and build up, just like when you climb up a ladder.

Read It

Read the poem out loud. Underline the high frequency words.

<u>The Noise</u> by Amy Posey

Clang! Clap! Bump!
What is it?
Stomp! Ding! Thump!
Is it the cat or the dog?
Yes! That is when I saw the cat jump on the lamp!
What a bang!

Draw a picture to go along with the poem above.

ACTIVITY GUIDE

Episode 210: Repurposing Plastic and -ough- Words
Book: *Plastic Eco Activities* by Louise Nelson

Scan below to watch lesson

Phonics Skills

Spelling Pattern **o-u-g-h**

When a word contains the spelling pattern **o-u-g-h**, those letters put together can represent seven different sounds. The chart on the right has words with four of the most common sounds.

Read the word on the left side of the chart. Listen to the ending sound. Read the word on the right side of the chart using the same ending sound from the first column for the o-u-g-h spelling pattern in the word.

Matching sounds	*Words with o-u-g-h*
no	although dough though
you	through
off	cough trough
stuff	enough rough tough

Reuse It

The book, *Plastic Eco Activities,* by Louise Nelson, shows us a couple of ideas for making games out of recycled materials.

PLASTIC PLAY!

These games are simple to make with paper, crayons, and bottle caps.

Bottle-cap Bingo!

Draw circles on a piece of paper. Color them in different colors. Put different colored bottle caps into a bag. Now, take turns picking out a bottle cap. If it matches a colored circle on your paper, place it on that circle. The first one to fill their piece of paper wins.

22

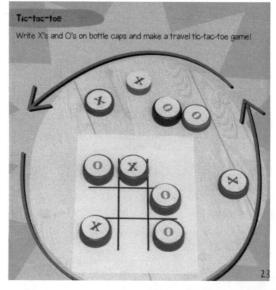

Tic-tac-toe

Write X's and O's on bottle caps and make a travel tic-tac-toe game!

23

Read, Write, ROAR!™ 2nd Grade Episode 210

ACTIVITY GUIDE

Episode 210: Closed and Open Syllables
Book: *Coyote's Soundbite: A Poem for our Planet* by John Agard

Scan below to watch lesson

Read It

A few years ago, lead was found in Flint's drinking water. Many kids got sick because they had been drinking the water for a long time. Some kids had skin issues and even changes to their brains, making it hard for them to learn. Furthermore, it's happening in Benton Harbor and many cities in Michigan right now!

Michigan needs to check its water to make sure kids are not being hurt from their drinking water. One child in one family is too many!

Foundational Skills

An **open syllable** is a special kind of syllable. Open syllables have one WRITTEN vowel that is NOT followed by one or more consonants. Open syllables USUALLY have vowels that make their long vowel sound.

Rules for Dividing Syllables

Every syllable has one vowel or vowel team.

-Place a dot under each vowel

-Underline any vowel teams,

-Divide between two consonants

Try It

Go through and underline each sentence in the text above according to the color code below:

Green = topic sentence

Yellow = important information

(story telling parts)

Blue = details (thoughts; feelings;

description sentences)

Think About It

Look at this word. Each syllable is written in a different color. Which syllable in this word is not "closed in" by a consonant or consonants at the end?

newspaper

The second syllable ends with the vowel Aa. It is an open syllable.

Compare the Length

Directions: Put the objects in order from shortest to longest. Label the shortest object 1, label the middle object 2, and label the longest object 3.

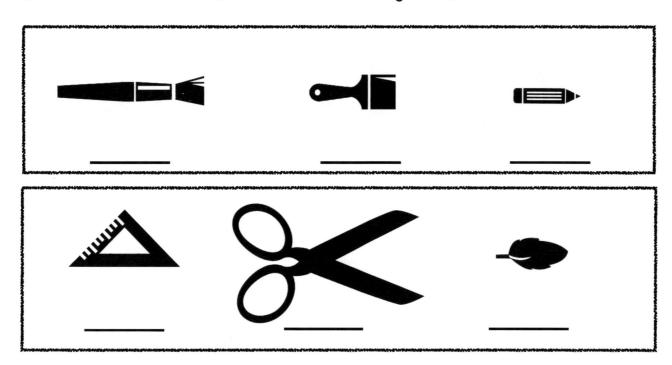

_____   _____   _____

_____   _____   _____

Directions: Compare the 3 objects below. Fill in the blanks to complete the sentence.

The _____ is taller than the _____ and

_____.

Split the Shape

Materials:
1. spinner (you will need a pencil and paperclip to create the spinner)
2. recording sheet
3. 2 players

Directions:
1. Player 1 spins and splits their shape.
2. Compare the shapes.
3. If you made equal parts, name the parts using halves, thirds, or fourths on the recording sheet.
4. Player 2 repeats steps 1-3. Continue taking turns until the recording sheet is filled in.

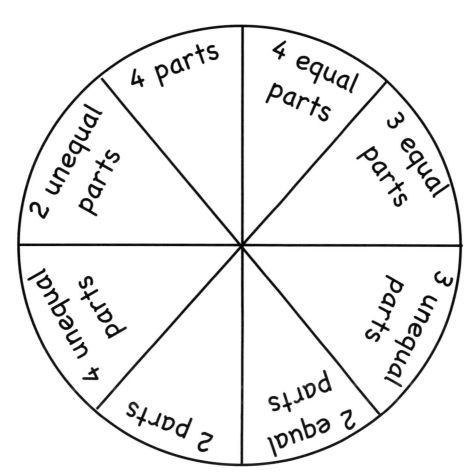

Math Mights 2nd Grade #311 | © Strategic Intervention Solutions, LLC | mathmights.org

 # Recording Sheet

Player 1	Player 2
☐	☐
▯	▯
◯	◯
▭	▭

Equivalent Fraction Roll

Materials: 6 dice

Directions:

1. Player 1 rolls 2 die and makes a fraction with the 2 amounts shown on the dice. If you roll any fives, they count as a wild card and can be any number you'd like.

2. Player 2 rolls 6 dice and tries to create a fraction that is equivalent to Player 1's fraction. (remember fives are wild)

3. If you cannot, re-roll as many number dice as you'd like. You can re-roll twice.

4. If you can make equivalent fractions, record your statement and show or explain how you know the fractions are equivalent.

5. You get 1 point for each pair of equivalent fractions you write.

6. Repeat steps 1-5 starting with Player 2. Play 8 rounds.

	Equivalent Fractions	If an equivalent fraction was created, circle the player who gets the point.		Equivalent Fractions	If an equivalent fraction was created, circle the player who gets the point.
Round 1	$\frac{\Box}{\Box} = \frac{\Box}{\Box}$	Player 1 or Player 2	Round 5	$\frac{\Box}{\Box} = \frac{\Box}{\Box}$	Player 1 or Player 2
Round 2	$\frac{\Box}{\Box} = \frac{\Box}{\Box}$	Player 1 or Player 2	Round 6	$\frac{\Box}{\Box} = \frac{\Box}{\Box}$	Player 1 or Player 2
Round 3	$\frac{\Box}{\Box} = \frac{\Box}{\Box}$	Player 1 or Player 2	Round 7	$\frac{\Box}{\Box} = \frac{\Box}{\Box}$	Player 1 or Player 2
Round 4	$\frac{\Box}{\Box} = \frac{\Box}{\Box}$	Player 1 or Player 2	Round 8	$\frac{\Box}{\Box} = \frac{\Box}{\Box}$	Player 1 or Player 2

Week 6: Great Outdoors

July 25-31

Explore the world outside your door and the incredible parks and waters that belong to us all.

Use the sheet below to mark off this week's activities as you complete them. See if you can get a BINGO!

Playlists this week: www.michiganlearning.org/greatoutdoors

Make a bird feeder (pg. 93)	60 mins. of activity	Read 20 minutes	Watch the sunset	Watch Read, Write, ROAR!
Read 20 minutes	Watch Math Mights	Search for Textured Treasures (pg. 91)	Visit a new place	60 mins. of activity
60 mins. of activity	Draw a pollinator (pg. 95)	HAVE FUN! (Free Space)	Try a new food	Read 20 minutes
Watch Read, Write, ROAR!	Go swimming	Watch Math Mights	Watch InPACT at Home	Make leaf rubbings (pg. 94)
Watch InPACT at Home	Read 20 minutes	Watch the sunrise	60 mins. of activity	Watch Live from the Opera House

Search for Textured Treasures!

From a prickly pinecone to a soft sweater, everything we touch has texture. How many textures can you find inside or outside of your house? Race the clock or race a friend with this printable scavenger hunt!

Instructions:

1) Look at the scavenger hunt table on the following page.

2) Begin hunting for textures on your list.

3) When you find something, draw a picture or write the object's name next to its matching texture.

TEXTURE describes the feel or appearance of an object or the material an object is made of.

More Ways to Play:

- Instead of drawing or writing, snap photos with a digital camera or camera phone.
- In the spaces on your sheet, make crayon rubbings of the textures you find.
- Target your scavenger hunt. Look for objects in nature, in your kitchen, or a specific room.
- Explore other senses. Find things with different colors, smells, or even tastes. (Tastes found in the kitchen, of course.)

Find more games and activities at **pbskidsforparents.org**

Funding for The Ruff Ruffman Show is provided by the Corporation for Public Broadcasting and the Department of Education. The contents of this document were developed under a cooperative agreement #PRU295A150003, from the U.S. Department of Education. However, these contents do not necessarily represent the policy of the Department of Education, and you should not assume endorsement by the Federal Government. Made available by the Corporation for Public Broadcasting, a private corporation funded by the American people. TM/© 2017 WGBH Educational Foundation. PBS KIDS® and the PBS KIDS® Logo are registered trademarks of PBS. Used with permission.

Corporation for Public Broadcasting

I spy something rough!

Name

I'm looking for something...	I found a...
smooth	
rough	
bumpy	
prickly	
sticky	
fluffy	
glossy	

Funding for The Ruff Ruffman Show is provided by the Corporation for Public Broadcasting and the Department of Education. The contents of this document were developed under a cooperative agreement #PRU295A150003, from the U.S. Department of Education. However, these contents do not necessarily represent the policy of the Department of Education, and you should not assume endorsement by the Federal Government. Made available by the Corporation for Public Broadcasting, a private corporation funded by the American people. TM/© 2017 WGBH Educational Foundation. PBS KIDS® and the PBS KIDS® Logo are registered trademarks of PBS. Used with permission.

  Corporation for Public Broadcasting

Make a Bird Feeder

What You Need:

- **Pinecone, paper towel holder or piece of bread**
- **Peanut butter or honey**
- **Your choice of the following:**
  - **Raisins**
  - **Cranberries**
  - **Plain popped popcorn**
  - **Sunflower seeds**
  - **Shelled plain peanuts**
  - **Mixed birdseed**
- **Safety scissors**
- **Wire, dental floss or cotton string**

What to Do:

1. Select a bird feeder base: Pinecones are a popular foundation for a bird feeder, but you may also use an empty paper towel roll or a stale piece of bread.

2. String it up: Run a wire, dental floss or cotton string through your bird feeder. Secure the two ends together to make a loop.

3. Make it sticky: Coat the base with peanut butter. If you know someone who has peanut allergies, use honey instead.

4. Add some goodies: Roll the feeder in raisins, cranberries, unsalted and unbuttered popcorn, sunflower seeds, shelled plain peanuts or mixed birdseed.

5. Hang it up: Place your bird feeder on a hook or on a tree branch outside your window. Discover which birds are popular in your neighborhood, research what they like to eat, and make a bird feeder for them.

6. Keep a wildlife journal: Record what kind of birds and other animals come to visit your feeder!

Find more games and activities at pbskidsforparents.org

Make Leaf and Bark Rubbings

Instructions

1. You'll need one or more crayons with the labels removed, some cardboard or a clip board and some masking tape to help hold leaves or bark in place.

2. When you're walking outside, collect a few fallen leaves, some bark or other natural materials. It's best if you find leaves or bark where you can feel bumps or ridges.

3. Once you've found your leaves, bark or other items, use tape to secure the edges of the leaves, bark or other materials to the clipboard or cardboard so that they will stay in place while you make your rubbing.

4. Place this paper over the leaves and bark and lightly rub the side of the crayon over the surface of the paper, just hard enough so that the texture shows.

5. Write a list of words to describe how the leaf or bark feels or looks like.

What You'll Need:

- **Trees**
- **Plain white paper**
- **Crayons with label removed**
- **Masking tape (optional)**
- **Cardboard or clipboard**
- **Paper bag for collecting leaves**

Find more games and activities at **pbskidsforparents.org**

FRIENDLY NEIGHBORHOOD POLLINATORS

POLINIZADORES AMISTOSOS DEL VECINDARIO

Pollinators help plants with flowers to grow. Go on a pollinator scavenger hunt! Take a walk around your neighborhood or in a local park. Look for the pollinators below. Draw a circle around each one that you see.

Los polinizadores ayudan a las plantas con flores a crecer. ¡Ve a una búsqueda de polinizadores! Da un paseo por tu vecindario o en un parque local. Busca los polinizadores de abajo. Dibuja un círculo alrededor de cada uno que veas.

Bats / Murciélagos

Bees / Abejas

Butterflies / Mariposas

Hummingbirds / Colibríes

Moths / Polillas

Beetles / Escarabajos

In the box below, draw a picture of one of the pollinators you saw. If there were plants nearby, put them in your drawing too! What kinds of plants do pollinators seem to like?

En el recuadro de abajo, dibuja uno de los polinizadores que viste. Si había plantas cerca, ¡dibújalas también! ¿Qué tipo de plantas parecen gustar a los polinizadores?

it's Storytime CHALLENGE

Growing Seeds

- Cardboard Egg Carton
- Scissors
- Potting Soil
- Used Coffee Grounds
- Seeds
- A Waterproof Plate or Tray

My Design Ideas:

How could I improve on my design for next time?

DID YOU KNOW?

Humans use more than 2000 different types of plants to create various delicious food items in our meals!

Seeds can be as tiny as a grain of sand or bigger than a fingernail.

POWER UP WORDS

- Seed
- Root · Stem
- Flower

CAREER LIFTOFF

- Gardener
- Farmer
- Florist
- Agricultural Engineer
- Forester

CITY OPERA HOUSE

TCAPS
Traverse City Area Public Schools
Great Community, Great Schools

Michigan LEARNING CHANNEL
A PUBLIC MEDIA PARTNERSHIP

LIVE ~from the~ OPERA HOUSE it's Storytime

Learning Standards: Kindergarten

K-LS1-1 Use observations to describe patterns of what plants and animals (including humans) need to survive.

K-ESS3-3: Communicate solutions that will reduce the impact of humans on the land, water, air, and/or other living things in the local environment.

ACTIVITY GUIDE

Episode 211: Astronaut Training
Book: *Astronaut Training* by Aneta Cruz

Scan below to watch lesson

Try It

Write or draw things in the diagram that you see in the Daytime on the left, and things you see in the Nighttime on the right. Things that you see in both day and night can go in the middle.

Daytime   Nighttime

Both

Draw It

In the story *Astronaut Training* by Aneta Cruz, Astrid dreams of becoming an astronaut.

Draw something that you dream of being when you grow up.

High Frequency Words

do

find

Be on the lookout for these words out and about and when reading or listening to a story. When you are writing, try to remember how you learned to spell them.

ACTIVITY GUIDE

Episode 211: Repurposing Metal and Simple Compound Words
Book: *Metal Eco Activities* by Louise Nelson

Scan below to watch lesson

Read It

A compound word is two smaller words that are joined together to make a new word.

out + side = outside

Pick two of the words from this word bank in order to create the compound word that matches the picture.

butter	bath	rain
coat	tub	fly

_____

_____

_____

Think About It

Properties of Metal:
• Can be thick or thin
• Made by people from a natural material
• Hard and strong
• Waterproof
• Opaque /NOT see-through
• Can be made into many shapes and colors

Take a look around you to see what materials made of metal you can find. Collect these materials and share them with someone in your home.

Try It

Create your own tin can telephone.

ACTIVITY GUIDE

Episode 212: Even More Closed and Open Syllables
Book: *Coyote's Soundbite: A Poem for our Planet* by John Agard

Scan below to watch lesson

Read It

An accurate reader pays close attention to every letter in a word.

Look at each word below. Think about the sounds that the letters make. Read the word out loud.

pan

pant

plant

Think About It

As you are reading a book, you may have different reactions to the words on the page. Sometimes you may feel happy while other times you may feel sad, angry, or confused.

After reading a book and experiencing different feelings, you can respond by writing a sentence that provides evidence from the book to backup your reaction.

Try It

Start at the bottom of the ladder. Follow the instructions to change each word. Write the word in the space provided.

Add a **d** at the end

Change the **f** to a **t**

Change the **v** to a **r**

Change the **d** to a **f**

dive

Write It

Use the sentence starters below to write about a book that you have read.

This book made me happy because

_____

_____

_____

This book made me think because

_____

_____

_____

Measuring with a Tool

Directions:

1. Choose an object to measure. Record the object on the chart below.
2. Choose a length measuring tool. You can use paperclips, cubes, etc.
3. Measure the length of the object with your tool and record the length on the chart below.
4. Repeat steps 1–3 five more times.

Object	Length
Example: pencil	6 paperclips

Clocks and Time

1. Sierra wakes up in the morning at 7:15. Show this time on the clock face below. Circle a.m. or p.m.

a.m. or p.m.

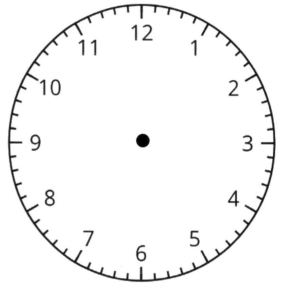

2. Sierra goes to bed at 8:45. Show this time on the clock face below. Circle a.m. or p.m.

a.m. or p.m.

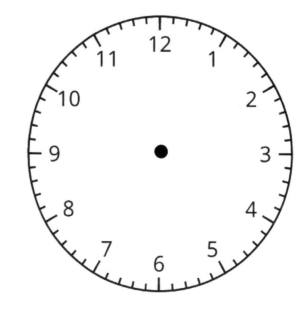

Write the time for each clock face.

3.

_____ : _____

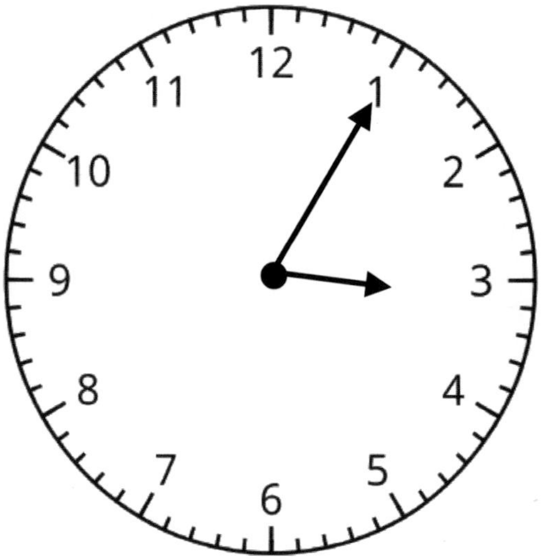

4.

_____ : _____

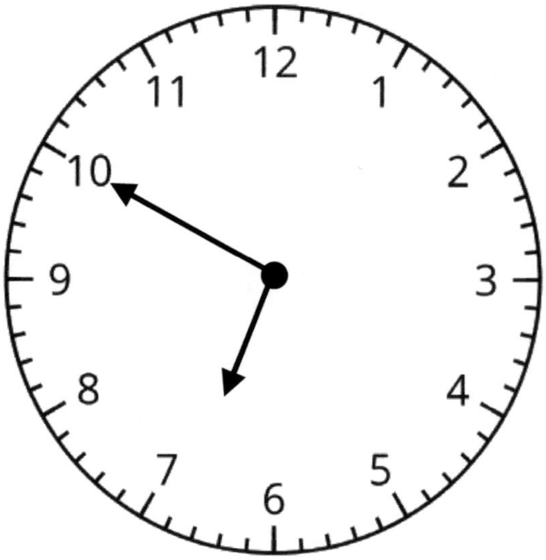

5.

_____ : _____

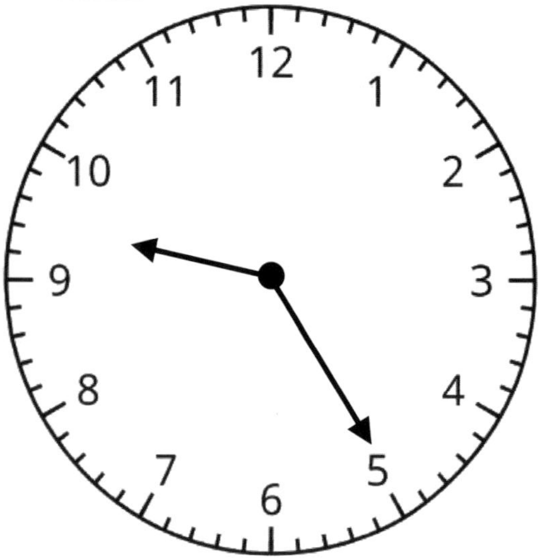

6.

_____ : _____

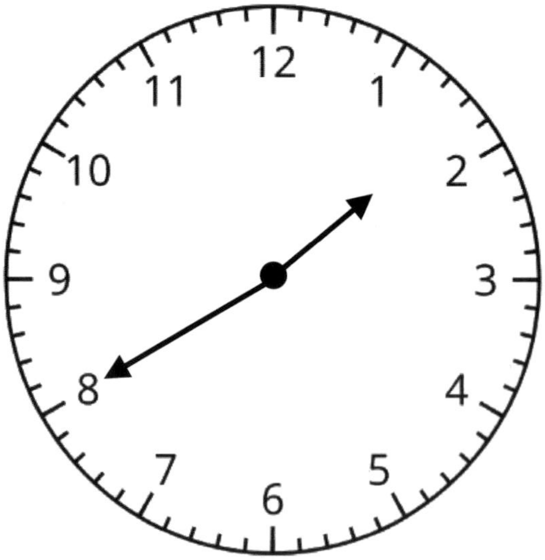

Math Mights 2nd Grade #314 | © Strategic Intervention Solutions, LLC | mathmights.org

Spin To Win!

Materials: make a spinner with a pencil and paperclip, 2 different color crayons, recording sheet

Directions:

1. Player 1 chooses a denominator for the first round: 2, 3, 4, 6, or 8.
2. Each player spins for the numerator of their fraction.
3. Use the recording sheet. Each player, locate and label your fractions on the same number line.
4. The greatest fraction wins and picks the denominator for the next round.
5. Repeat for 5 rounds. The player who wins the most rounds, wins the game.

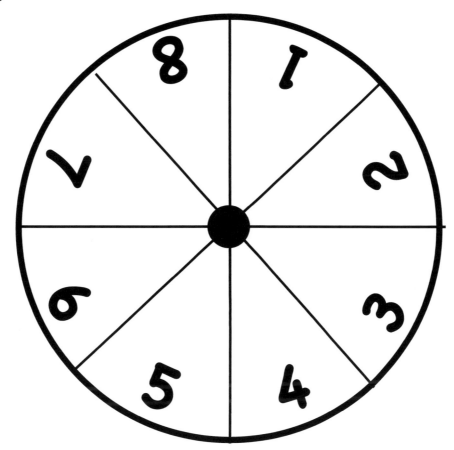

Recording Sheet

	Locate and label your fraction (each player use a different color).	
Round 1	⊢———⊢———⊢———⊢ 1 2 3 4	☐/☐ — ☐/☐
Round 2	⊢———⊢———⊢———⊢ 1 2 3 4	☐/☐ — ☐/☐
Round 3	⊢———⊢———⊢———⊢ 1 2 3 4	☐/☐ — ☐/☐
Round 4	⊢———⊢———⊢———⊢ 1 2 3 4	☐/☐ — ☐/☐
Round 5	⊢———⊢———⊢———⊢ 1 2 3 4	☐/☐ — ☐/☐

Math Mights 3rd Grade #318 | © Strategic Intervention Solutions, LLC | mathmights.org

Week 7: When I Grow Up   August 1-7

All summer we'll learn about different careers—this week, think about all the exciting possibilities in your future!

Use the sheet below to mark off this week's activities as you complete them. See if you can get a BINGO!

Playlists this week: www.michiganlearning.org/growup

Learn about a family member's job	60 mins. of activity	Read 20 minutes	Try Bianca's body math (pg. 107)	Watch Read, Write, ROAR!
Read 20 minutes	Watch Math Mights	Watch Live from the Opera House	Practice ballet positions (pg. 106)	60 mins. of activity
60 mins. of activity	Draw a self portrait	HAVE FUN! (Free Space)	Learn about a family member's job	Read 20 minutes
Watch Read, Write, ROAR!	Watch Meet the Helpers	Watch Math Mights	Watch InPACT at Home	Fill in the compost fractions (pg. 110)
Watch InPACT at Home	Read 20 minutes	Practice Fact Families (pg. 109)	60 mins. of activity	Invent an instrument (pg. 108)

In 2015, Misty Copeland became the first Black principal ballerina with the American Ballet Theater. Learn the five basic foot positions used in ballet. Create a dance using the positions and add leaping and twirling to your moves just like Misty!

The Five Ballet Positions

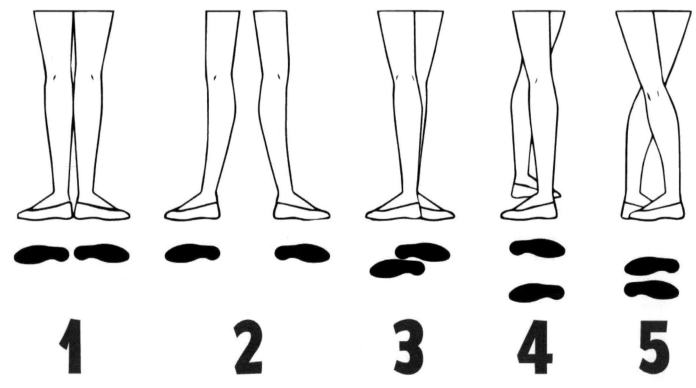

Find more games and activities at **pbskidsforparents.org**

Corporation for Public Broadcasting

Bianca's Body Math

Did you know that for a lot of people, their foot is the same length as their forearm? Find out if it's true for you!

YOU NEED

piece of string (a little longer than your height)
black marker

DIRECTIONS

First, start at the end of your string and mark off seven of your foot-lengths.

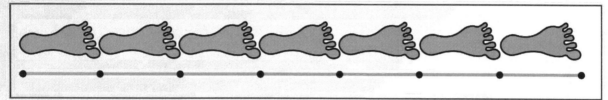

Now use the string to measure the body parts listed below. Have a friend help. Be sure to measure from one black mark on the string to the next.

Measure	About how many foot lengths?
From wrist to elbow (forearm)	_____
Around widest part of your fist	_____
Around your forehead	_____
From head to toe	_____

Who Knew?

A person's height is often the same as his or her arm span (arms out to side, middle fingertip to middle fingertip). Is yours?

Music to Our Ears!

Help! Hacker stole all the musical instruments from the borgs in R-Fair City on the day of their big parade! Can you invent a musical instrument to save the parade?

Materials

For your Music Maker:

❏ plastic and paper cups, paper plates, beans, beads, jingle bells, paper towel rolls, pipe cleaners, paper straws, waxed paper, combs, rubber bands, balloons, craft sticks, plastic salad bar containers, aluminum foil, and other found objects

❏ Masking tape

❏ Stapler

❏ "My Invention Design" handout

❏ Pencil

Make Your Instrument

1 Play with the materials. Find sounds that you like by shaking, striking, or spinning objects.

2 Use the "My Invention Design" handout to plan your Music Maker. Make a sketch to show what it looks like.

3 Make your instrument and try it out. Does it work the way you planned?

4 What changes can you make to your instrument to improve how it sounds?

How Am I Inventing?

Inventors take time to plan an invention before they start building. They start with an idea of what they want their invention to do and make a plan. When they stick to that plan, they can build an invention that works the way they want. This is called *designing for function*. When you design your instrument to make a particular sound, you're designing for function, too.

Get inventive with CYBERCHASE on PBS KIDS GO!
Check local listings or visit www.pbskidsgo.org/cyberchase.

CYBERCHASE is produced by Thirteen / WNET New York and Nelvana Limited.
Major funding for CYBERCHASE is provided by the National Science Foundation, Ernst & Young LLP, Northrop Grumman Corporation, Intel Corporation, Intel Foundation, PBS and the Corporation for PublicBroadcasting. Additional funding is provided by The Volckhausen Family.

Page 1

Agents, Villains, and Fact Families

The Odd Squad Mobile Unit must stop a group of villains from causing oddness! Help the agents solve the **fact family** problems shown in the triangles below and on the next page. A fact family is a group of numbers related to one another. Use addition and subtraction to find the answers and help end the oddness that is taking over the city!

Here's a fact family using the numbers **1**, **2**, and **3**.

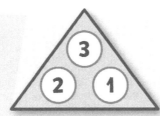

$$2 + 1 = 3 \qquad 1 + 2 = 3$$
$$3 - 2 = 1 \qquad 3 - 1 = 2$$

This example shows the fact family for the numbers **3**, **4**, and **7**.

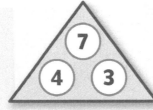

$$4 + 3 = 7 \qquad 3 + 4 = 7$$
$$7 - 3 = 4 \qquad 7 - 4 = 3$$

Can you finish this fact family?

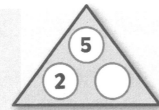

$$2 + \square = 5 \qquad \square + 2 = 5$$
$$5 - 2 = \square \qquad 5 - \square = 2$$

Create another fact family with the number **5**, but don't use the numbers **0**, **2**, or **3** in the triangle.

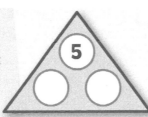

$$\square + \square = 5 \qquad \square + \square = 5$$
$$5 - \square = \square \qquad 5 - \square = \square$$

Funded by:

Find Odd Squad games, videos, and OddTube at pbskids.org/oddsquad

COMPOST FRACTIONS

FRACCIONES DE COMPOSTAJE

Composting is the process of changing food waste (and grass and leaves) into new soil. To compost, you need to use 1/3 "green" material (fruit and vegetable scraps) and 2/3 "brown" material (dried leaves and recycled paper).

1. Count the squares below. Each one is 1/3 of the total rectangle.

2. Color 1/3 of the rectangle below (or 1 square) with a green crayon or marker.

3. Color 2/3 of the rectangle below (or 2 squares) with a brown crayon or marker.

El compostaje es el proceso por el cual los residuos de alimentos (el césped y las hojas, también) se transforman en un tipo especial de tierra. Para hacer compost, se necesita 1/3 de material "verde" (restos de frutas y verduras) y 2/3 de material "marrón" (hojas secas y papel reciclado).

1. Cuenta los cuadrados de abajo. Cada uno es 1/3 de todo el rectángulo.

2. Colorea 1/3 del rectángulo de abajo (o 1 cuadrado) con un crayón o marcador verde.

3. Colorea 2/3 del rectángulo de abajo (o 2 cuadrados) con un crayón o marcador marrón.

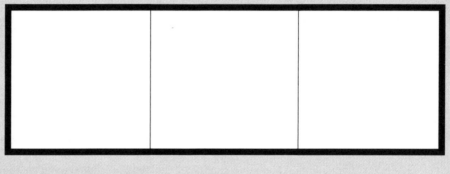

Let's find more ways to show this rule. If you had three balls, how many green balls and how many brown balls would you need?

Veamos más formas de mostrar esta regla. Si tuvieras tres pelotas, ¿cuántas pelotas verdes y cuántas pelotas marrones tendrías?

What if you had six balls?

¿Y si tuvieras seis pelotas?

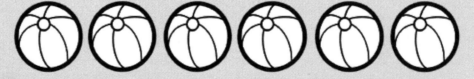

it's Storytime CHALLENGE

Protect Your Egg

- **A Raw Egg**
- **Foam**
- **Duct tape**
- **Masking tape**
- **White paper**
- **Colored Pencils**
- **Crayons**

My Design Ideas:

How could I improve on my design for next time?

POWER UP WORDS

Iteration
Kinetic energy
Potential energy

DID YOU KNOW?

A sports engineer focuses on preventing injury while enhancing the performance of the athletes. That includes what the athlete wears and uses, but also the sporting environment and the tools for analyzing the athlete's performance!

CAREER LIFTOFF

› Industrial Designer
› Physical Therapist
› Sports Technologist
› Simulation Engineer

Learning Standards: 3rd-5th Grade

3-5-ETS1-1. Define a simple design problem reflecting a need or a want that includes specified criteria for success and constraints on materials, time, or cost.

CITY OPERA HOUSE

TCAPS
Traverse City Area Public Schools
Great Community, Great Schools

Michigan LEARNING CHANNEL
A PUBLIC MEDIA PARTNERSHIP

LIVE ~from the~ OPERA HOUSE it's Storytime

ACTIVITY GUIDE

Episode 213: The Stars and S-Blends

Scan below to watch lesson

Word Ladder

Help us climb the word ladder! Follow the directions and write each word on the rungs of the ladder. Read each word you write.

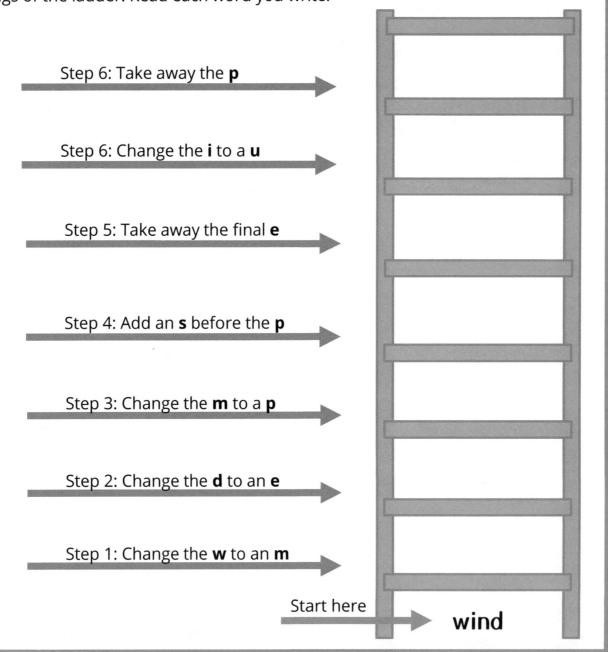

Step 6: Take away the **p**

Step 6: Change the **i** to a **u**

Step 5: Take away the final **e**

Step 4: Add an **s** before the **p**

Step 3: Change the **m** to a **p**

Step 2: Change the **d** to an **e**

Step 1: Change the **w** to an **m**

Start here → **wind**

ACTIVITY GUIDE

Episode 214: Comparing Texts and Making Words
Book: *The Water Walker* by Joanne Robinson

Scan below to watch lesson

Compare It

Choose two fiction books to read and then fill in the chart below.

Comparing Literature		
Title of Book 1	Story Elements	Title of Book 2
	Setting	
	Characters	
	Problem	
	Solution	

Phonics Skills

Let's make and read words as we move up the word ladder. Start at the bottom. Read the word **sister**. Remember that we can split words with more than one syllable between consonants **(sis/ter)** to make them easier to read. Follow the directions to see how to change the first syllable in each word as you move up the ladder. Each time you make a new word, practice reading and writing it before moving further up the ladder.

Change **crit** to **chap**

Change **af** to **crit**

Change **win** to **af**

Change **sis** to **win**

sister

Think About It

Using the information you filled out in the chart above, answer the following questions.

How are the two books alike?
How are the two books different?

ACTIVITY GUIDE

Episode 213: Closed, Open, and V-C-E
Part 1
Book: *Ajijaak ("Crane")* by Cecilia Rose
LaPointe

Scan below to watch lesson

Foundational Skills

Asking questions while reading a book can deepen your understanding of the story. Use the chart below to write questions as you are reading. Go back and reread parts of your book to answer your questions. Write your answers below your question. Be sure to include the page number where you found your answer.

Who	
What	
Where	
When	
Why	
How	

Sort Solid Shapes

Directions:

1. Cut out the labels below. Figure out which box represents each label. Glue down the labels in the correct box.

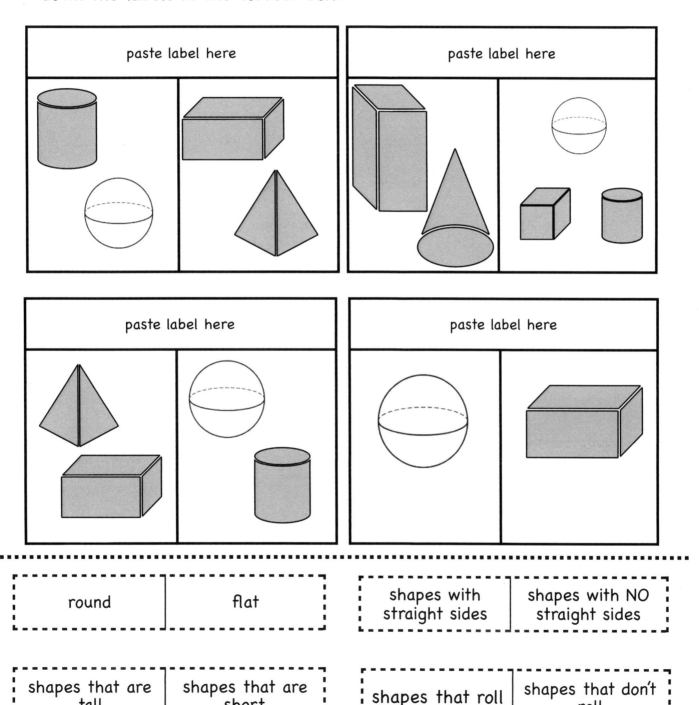

This page was left blank to cut out the activity on the other side.

Measure to the Nearest Half or Quarter Inch

Directions:

1. Label one ruler with halves and cut it out.
2. Find 5 objects and use this ruler to measure the objects to the nearest half-inch.
3. Record your measurements on the recording sheet.
4. Label the second ruler with fourths (quarters) and cut it out.
5. Find 5 objects and use this ruler to measure the objects to the nearest quarter-inch.
6. Record your measurements on the recording sheet.

0 inches
1
2
3
4
5
6
7
8
9

This page was left blank to cut out the activity on the other side.

Recording Sheet

Object	Measurement to the nearest half-inch.

Object	Measurement to the quarter half-inch.

Coin Compare

Materials: money cards (cut out)

Directions:
1. Put all the cards in one pile face down.
2. Player 1 and Player 2 each turn over a card from the top of the pile.
3. Each player finds the value of the collection of coins shown on their card.
4. Both players compare their cards. The player with the greatest coin value takes both cards.
5. Continue to play until all the cards have been taken from the pile.
6. The player with the most cards wins!

	Player 1	Player 2	Which player has the greatest value?
1	_____ ¢	_____ ¢	
2	_____ ¢	_____ ¢	
3	_____ ¢	_____ ¢	
4	_____ ¢	_____ ¢	
5	_____ ¢	_____ ¢	
6	_____ ¢	_____ ¢	
7	_____ ¢	_____ ¢	
8	_____ ¢	_____ ¢	
9	_____ ¢	_____ ¢	
10	_____ ¢	_____ ¢	

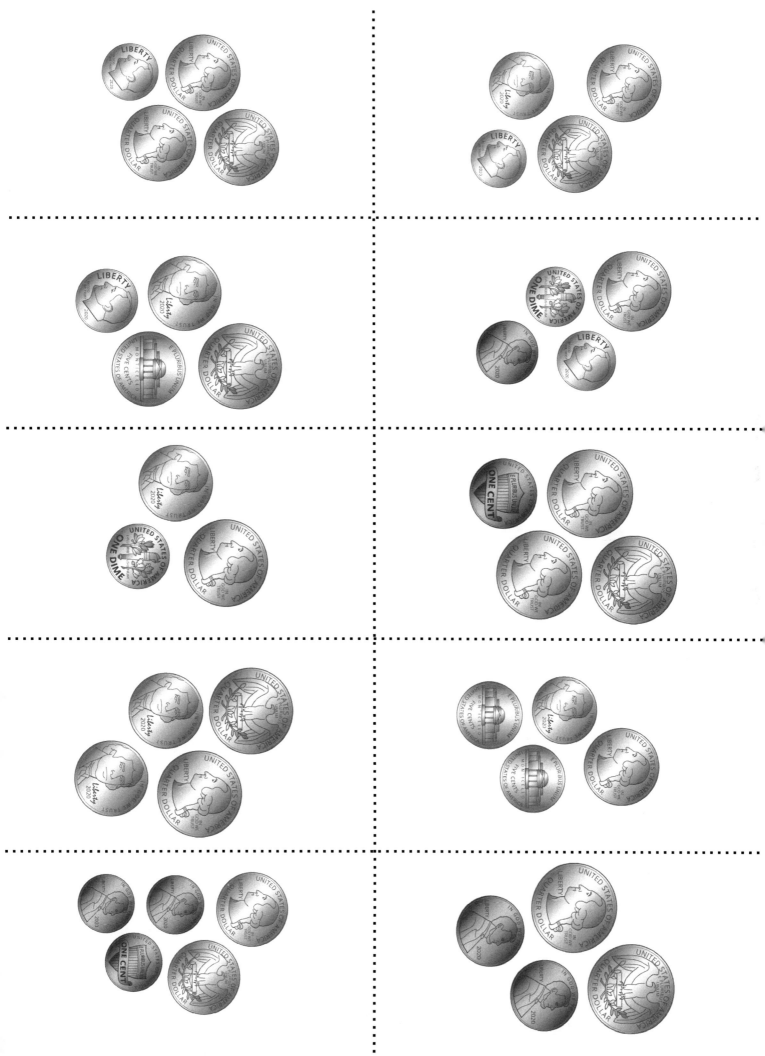

This page was left blank to cut out the activity on the other side.

Week 8: Shoot for the Stars   August 8-14

Look up at the night sky and into outer space and meet people who risked everything to follow their dreams.

Use the sheet below to mark off this week's activities as you complete them. See if you can get a BINGO!

Playlists this week: www.michiganlearning.org/stars

Stargaze	60 mins. of activity	Read 20 minutes	Watch Live from the Opera House	Watch Read, Write, ROAR!
Read 20 minutes	Watch Math Mights	Watch the sunset	Try Luna's word find (pg. 128)	60 mins. of activity
60 mins. of activity	Make a poster (pg. 129)	HAVE FUN! (Free Space)	Look at the clouds	Read 20 minutes
Watch Read, Write, ROAR!	Draw a space creature (pg. 124)	Watch Math Mights	Watch InPACT at Home	Visit a new place
Watch InPACT at Home	Read 20 minutes	Stargaze	60 mins. of activity	Make flashlight constellations

SPACE CREATURE

Draw a space creature's head here!

Have a friend draw its body here.

Then you draw its legs and feet here.

Produced by WGBH Kids for PBS. Funded by the Corporation for Public Broadcasting. © 2019 WGBH Educational Foundation. Based on Scribbles and Ink books written by Ethan Long, published by Harriet Ziefert, Inc., underlying Scribbles and Ink characters and artwork are copyrights and trademarks of Ethan Long.

pbskids.org

Flashlight Constellations

A constellation is a series of stars that form a picture in the sky. Astronomers use it today to help pinpoint the locations of other stars. Ask an adult to help cut out the four constellations and punch small holes on each star. These points are the locations of the stars in each constellation.

Choose the size circle that fits on your flashlight lens, cutting along the inner or outer dashed circle. Flip the picture so it's facing the flashlight.

Point the light to a dark surface and look at the constellation that shines through. One at a time, identify each constellation and talk about how you identified them.

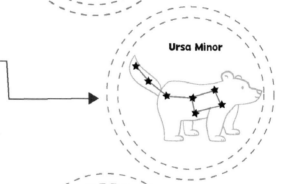

Ursa Major

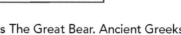

URSA MAJOR

Ursa Major is also known as The Great Bear. Ancient Greeks tell the story about a beautiful girl named Callisto who was turned into a bear by a mean goddess. A tracker tried to catch the bear, but the Greek God Zeus saved Callisto by placing her up in the night sky where she was safe.

Ursa Minor

URSA MINOR

The story of Ursa Minor, or The Little Bear, comes from the Ancient Greeks. Arcas was a great hunter. One day while hunting in the woods, he came across a great bear. Little did he know that was actually his mother, Callisto, who was under a spell. Arcas was about to catch the great bear, but the Greek god Zeus, stopped him just in time and turned Arcas into a little bear so he could be with his mom. Zeus placed the two bears into the sky to keep them safe and protected.

Leo

LEO THE LION

In Greek myths, Leo the Lion lived outside an ancient city called Nemea. For many years, Leo would scoop up people from Nemea and no one would stop him. One day, Hercules went to stop the lion and won. Everyone who the lion had caught was set free. Zeus made Leo a constellation in the night sky to remind people of the story of Hercules and Leo.

TAURUS THE BULL

The Ancient Greeks tell the story of a wild bull named Taurus who had a bad temper. One day he trampled a field of wild flowers and Persephone, the Goddess of Spring, got very sad. Taurus apologized and they soon became good friends. From then on, every spring, Persephone would ride on Taurus' back and the two of them would make the flowers bloom as they walked by.

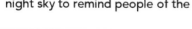
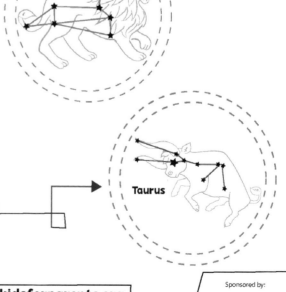

Taurus

WIND DANCER
FILMS

Find more games and activities at pbskidsforparents.org

Sponsored by:
ABCmouse.com®

The contents of this document were developed under a cooperative agreement (PR/Award No. U295A150003, CFDA No. 84.295A) from the U.S. Department of Education. However, these contents do not necessarily represent the policy of the Department of Education, and you should not assume endorsement by the Federal Government. © 2021 Jet Propulsion, LLC. Ready Jet Go! and the Ready Jet Go! logo are registered trademarks of Jet Propulsion, LLC. The PBS KIDS logo and PBS KIDS ® PBS. Used with permission. Corporate Funding is provided by ABCmouse.com. Made available by the Corporation for Public Broadcasting, a private corporation funded by the American people.

This page was left blank to cut out the activity on the other side.

Flashlight Constellations

Constellation Key

URSA MAJOR
The Great Bear

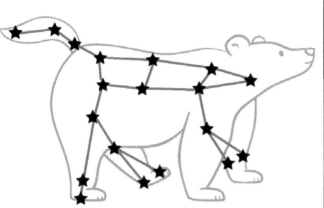

URSA MINOR
The Little Bear

LEO
The Lion

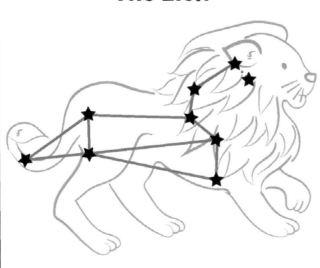

TAURUS
The Bull

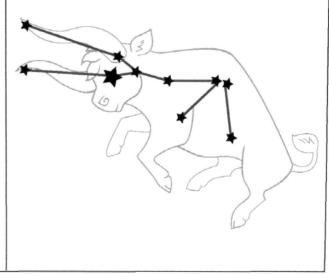

Word Find

Andy, Carmen, and Leo are traveling the world! Can you find all of these words?

J	M	T	R	A	V	E	L
F	R	I	E	N	D	S	C
E	K	L	U	N	A	S	E
H	R	Z	T	D	F	B	R
L	O	V	L	W	O	C	M
Q	D	R	Y	L	T	J	O
R	O	G	G	T	B	D	O
W	X	A	T	A	W	M	N

WORLD	LUNA	FRIENDS
TRAVEL	MOON	GLOBE

Find more games and activities at pbskids.org/luna

Produced by:

Sponsored by:

 # Big Finale

 BIG IDEA

There is a lot that we can do to impact the environment. What issues are important to you? Think about what you have learned and take the time to share things you can do to support and protect nature in our communities.

 WATCH

Watch the clip from *Space Waste Odyssey* where the CyberSquad and Motherboard share what they've learned about creating less trash with the citizens of Cyberspace.

- Remember that the CyberSquad noticed a lot of trash was building up in "trash patches" in Cyberspace. They examined the trash to find out what was causing the problem.
- After watching, think about what environmental issue was important to the CyberSquad and what they did about it:
  - What was the problem that the CyberSquad saw?
  - What was one way that they thought people in Cyber-space could fix that problem?
  - How did they spread the word about making less trash to other people?
  - Why is it important for the CyberSquad to share what they've learned with other people?

 EXPLORE: Use Your Voice

Materials:

- **Research materials to learn more about a topic**
- **Art materials for posters or digital materials** (like a cell phone camera or a blog post)

Instructions:

1. What is an environmental problem that exists in your school, neighborhood, or at home? Which issues are less well-known by your family, friends, or neighbors?
2. Decide on one (or a few) key issues for your community.
3. Brainstorm ways to share the information you've learned with as many people as possible. Examples include short video Public Service Announcements (you can use a cell phone camera), a page for the school website, articles for a school newspaper or blog, or posters for public spaces.
4. Create! Focus on including information about *why the issue matters* and *what people can do to help*. Then show off what you made!

it's Storytime CHALLENGE

Balloon Bagpipe

- Large Balloon
- Plastic Tube
- Plastic Bottle Top
- Scissors
- Tape

My Design Ideas:

How could I improve on my design for next time?

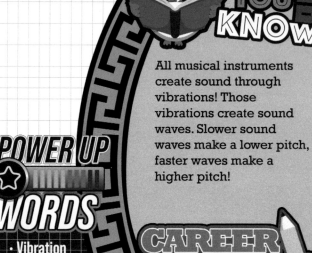

DID YOU KNOW?

All musical instruments create sound through vibrations! Those vibrations create sound waves. Slower sound waves make a lower pitch, faster waves make a higher pitch!

POWER UP WORDS

- Vibration
- Pitch
- Waves

CAREER LIFTOFF

- Musician
- Sound Engineer
- Music Director
- Teacher
- DJ

Learning Standards: 1st Grade
1-PS4-1 Plan and conduct investigations to provide evidence that vibrating materials can make sound and that sound can make materials vibrate.
K-2-ETS1-2 Develop a simple sketch, drawing, or physical model to illustrate how the shape of an object helps it function as needed to solve a given problem.
K-2-ETS1-1 Ask questions, make observations, and gather information about a situation people want to change to define a simple problem that can be solved through the development of a new or improved object or tool.

CITY OPERA HOUSE

TCAPS
Traverse City Area Public Schools
Great Community, Great Schools

Michigan LEARNING CHANNEL
A PUBLIC MEDIA PARTNERSHIP

LIVE from the OPERA HOUSE
it's Storytime

ACTIVITY GUIDE

Episode 216: Our Round, Round World and Plurals
Book: *It's a Round, Round World* by Ellie Peterson

Scan below to watch lesson

Mystery Word

A **noun** identifies a person place, thing or idea.
A **singular** noun names one person place, thing or idea, while a **plural** noun names more than one person, place, thing or idea.

Most singular nouns need an **'s'** at the end to become **plural**.
For example,
Singular (1): dog
Plural (more than 1): dog**s**

Regular singular nouns ending in 's', 'ss', 'sh', 'ch', 'x', or 'z' need an **'es'** at the end to become plural.
For example,
Singular (1): glass
Plural (more than 1): glass**es**

Try It

A **constellation** is a group of stars that forms a shape or picture. Connect the dots to see the Big Dipper Constellation shape.

1 2 3 4 5 6 7

Try It

-s or -es?
Practice making the following nouns plural by adding -s or -es. Remember to look at the ending to decide.
*Words ending with 's', 'ss', 'sh', 'ch', 'x', or 'z' need an '**es**'*

brush___   can__
tent___   bus__
hand__   mess__
pen__   lunch__
box__   pin__

Try It

Observation means to notice or see, or watch or listen carefully.
Find somewhere where you can use your senses to make some observations. Write what you hear 👂, see 👀, smell 👃, or feel ✋.

_____

_____

_____

_____

_____

Michigan Learning Channel

Read, Write, ROAR!™ 1st Grade Episode 216
Summer Fun Activity Book | **Elementary** | Michigan Learning Channel | **131**

ACTIVITY GUIDE

Episode 215: Protecting Our Planet

Scan below to watch lesson

Read It

Read the following passage out loud. Underline the compound words.

Yesterday, in art class, we were making posters out of cardboard. We used markers, magazines, and watercolor paints. Our posters were all about reducing, reusing, and recycling. We brainstormed ideas on the whiteboard and on notebook paper. When we finished, we posted our classwork in the hallways, the lunchroom, and on the playground.

Read It

Choose one compound word that you underlined above. Write each word that makes up the compound word on a blank below. Rewrite the word from the paragraph on the next line..

_____ + _____
　　word　　　　　　word

_____

Is this word a simple or complex compound word?

Words to Know

Compound Word - a word that is made up of two or more smaller words

Types of Compound Words:

A **simple compound word** has two syllables
sun + shine = sunshine

A **complex compound word** has *more* than two syllables.

after + noon = afternoon

Try It

Design your own tee shirt to promote reducing, reusing, and recycling.

ACTIVITY GUIDE

Episode 215: Closed, Open, and V-C-E Part 3
Book: *Greta and the Giants* by Zoe Tucker

Scan below to watch lesson

Think About It

When you are reading a story, think about the way the characters act. What patterns and behaviors do they display?

A character's behaviors and patterns help us make predictions and infer the kind of person they are using our schema (background information).

Foundational Skills

Character theory is the name of the character + your thoughts about the character + evidence in the book that provides support for your thoughts.

Try It

Use the graphic organizer below to create a **character theory** about a character in a book that you are reading.

Who is the character?

How does the character act? (patterns and behaviors)

_____ is _____ because

_____.

_____ is _____ because

_____.

_____ is _____ because

_____.

Draw Triangles, Rectangles, and Squares

Draw 3 triangles.

Draw 3 non-triangles.

Draw 3 rectangles.

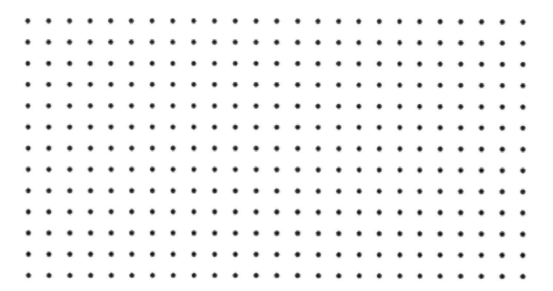

Draw 3 non-rectangles.

Draw 3 squares.

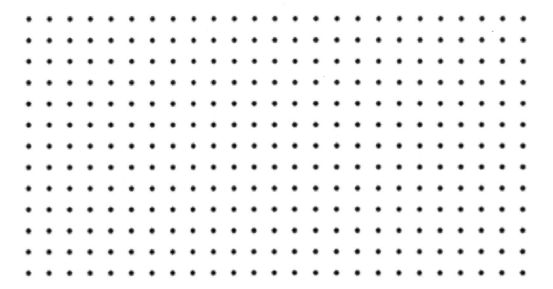

Draw 3 non-squares.

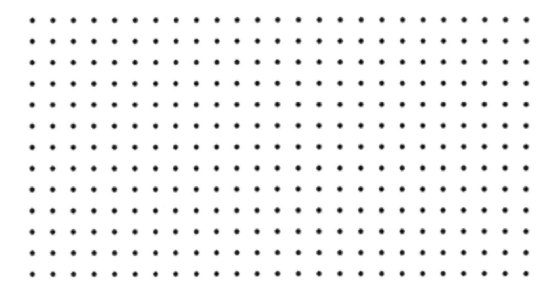

The Toy Store

Look at the prices of the toys, then answer the questions on the following page.

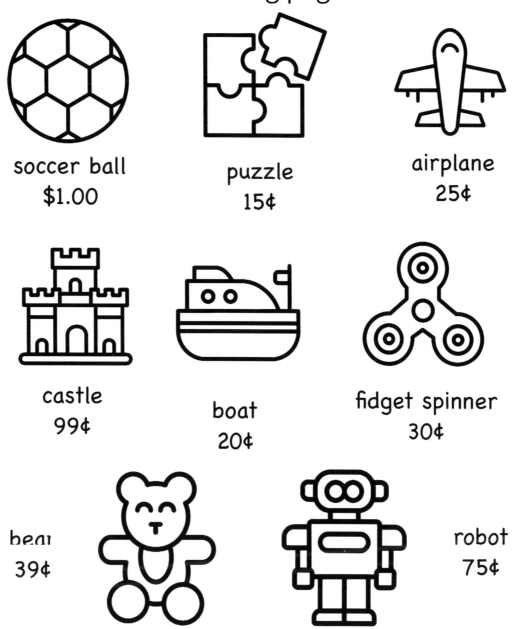

soccer ball
$1.00

puzzle
15¢

airplane
25¢

castle
99¢

boat
20¢

fidget spinner
30¢

bear
39¢

robot
75¢

I bought three robots and a soccer ball. How much did I spend?

I bought two toys and spent 40¢. What might I have bought?

I bought a castle and a fidget spinner and gave the shopkeeper 6 quarters. How much change did I receive?

You buy a boat and four airplanes. How much do you spend?

Ben buys 2 robots and a puzzle. How much change will he get from a 5 dollar bill?

I buy one bear and two castles. How much do I spend?

Choose any one item from the store. Show what coins you could use to pay the exact cost.

Choose any two items from the store. Show what coins you could use to pay the exact cost.

You buy five puzzles. How much change do you get from a one dollar bill?

I spent $1.19 at The Toy Store. What might I have bought?

Interpret Data From a Line Plot

Directions: Select **ALL** of the statements that are true about the measurements in the line plot below.

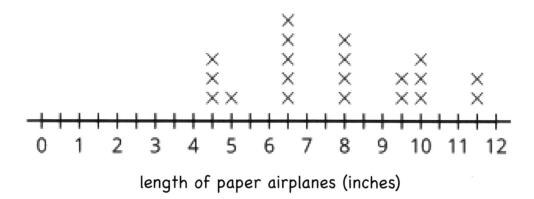

length of paper airplanes (inches)

A. 5 paper airplanes had a length of $6\frac{1}{2}$ inches.

B. 6 paper airplanes had a length of $9\frac{1}{2}$ inches.

C. There were 12 paper airplanes measured.

D. There were 20 paper airplanes measured.

E. The shortest paper airplane was 5 inches.

F. The shortest paper airplane was $4\frac{1}{2}$ inches.

SPECIAL THANKS TO OUR
MICHIGAN LEARNING CHANNEL FUNDERS:

The State of Michigan

Elaine and Leo Stern Foundation

The Donald and Mary Kosch Foundation